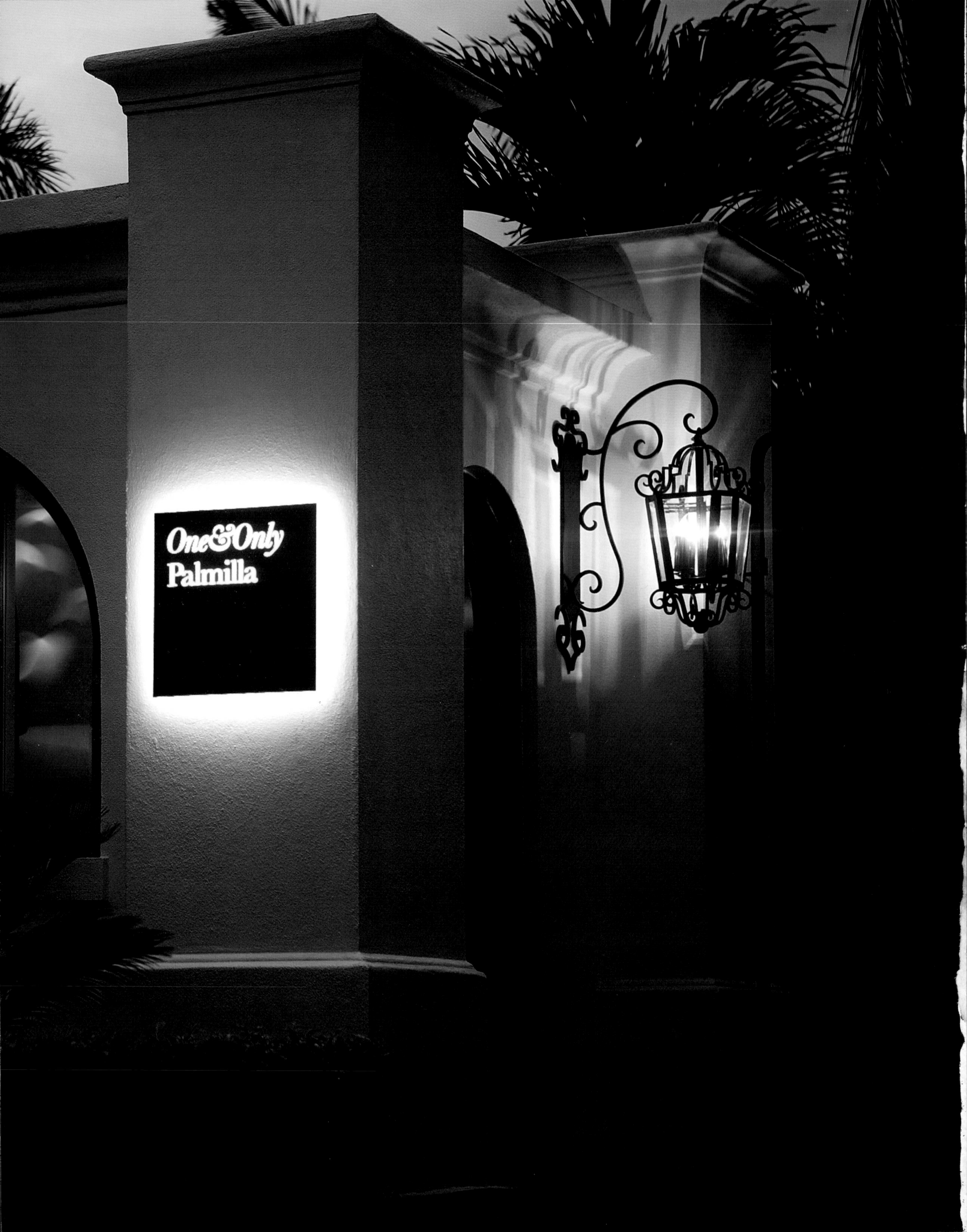
One&Only
Palmilla

One&Only
Palmilla

Spa Cuisine
by Charlie Trotter

One&Only
Palmilla

Spa Cuisine
by Charlie Trotter

RECIPES BY

CHARLIE TROTTER

AND

SARI ZERNICH

FOREWORD BY

EDWARD T. STEINER

NUTRITIONAL ANALYSIS BY

MARY ABBOTT HESS

WINE NOTE BY

ROCHELLE SMITH

PHOTOGRAPHY BY

KIPLING SWEHLA

I love great food. It's a fact of my life. I have traveled the world in search of new and different cuisines, and I find inspiration in nearly every food I try, from a single delicate herb garnishing an entrée in France to the most profound combination of ingredients on a dinner plate in Spain. Simply put, food that looks wonderful is food that I want to taste!

Of course, food must first and foremost be about what tastes good. "Flavor first" is how I like to think about eating. But presentation—the visual expression of food—is a close second. Indeed, I believe that most people eat as much with their eyes as they do with their palate.

When I travel, whether for business or pleasure, there are times when I like to eat healthy. I don't mean bland, boring food, such as huge plates heaped with salad greens. Instead, I seek out flavorful combinations that not only taste good but are also good for you. I know that many of our guests at One&Only Palmilla feel the same way. While some of them come here for a retreat from their busy lives, others are looking for a vacation filled with spa activities and healthy eating.

Once we completed our award-winning indoor-outdoor spa, I knew that the way to seal a memorable guest experience was to ensure that we had a unique spa cuisine program. That's when I challenged my friend Charlie Trotter to develop food that was both delicious and healthful. I had no idea that he would come up with the truly memorable dishes that he did!

The food he has created is unlike any spa cuisine I have ever eaten. Trust me, I have been to many spas and first-class resorts all over the world, and I have never encountered anything like the dishes served at One&Only Palmilla. Even though many of our guests are not here for spa or health-related vacations, they are still ordering this unique food because it tastes so appealing. The presentations are stunning, too—exactly what you would expect from a Charlie Trotter experience.

Our spa cuisine program has selections for breakfast, lunch, and dinner. Additionally, our resort guests, who are typically made up of an international who's who, all have different health and dietary goals. So I asked Charlie to ensure that his food would be flexible enough to meet many different needs. The result is something for everyone. Whether a guest wants low carb, no sugar, high protein, or low calorie, or any combination of those restrictions, he or she can find it at One&Only Palmilla.

I could eat this spa cuisine every day because it tastes so good, without ever thinking about how healthy it is for me. I know that our guests feel the same way, so Charlie and I decided to put together this collection of some of the recipes we serve here. That way, our guests can relive part of what they experienced after they arrive back home.

I hope you can visit us at One&Only Palmilla and enjoy this amazing spa cuisine firsthand. Look upon the recipes and images in the following pages as your invitation to an unforgettable moment in your life.

EDWARD T. STEINER
REGIONAL VICE PRESIDENT AND MANAGING DIRECTOR, ONE&ONLY PALMILLA

Sensuality. That single word captures everything I do, everything I seek to do, when it comes to cuisine. It embraces not just the art of creating cuisine, but more important, the art of experiencing cuisine. For example, when I look at a firm, ripe Donut peach, I immediately begin to imagine the countless possibilities of expression that its flavor offers. How do I seduce all there is from that luscious piece of fruit in a way that allows for multiple feelings once it hits the palate? Will I keep it whole and firm, or will I caress it with an herb oil and then carefully slice it and incorporate it into a main course? Each approach yields a very different effect in the mouth, so I have to decide what "ultimate expression" I want my guests to experience. That decision is what drives my creative process.

My approach to cuisine is essentially about the palate and becoming one with foods. I have often said that if I were any more obsessed with food, it would be perverse. I believe that you have to love what you are doing, and if you do, it is simple to do things at never-before-seen levels. Simply put, I am in love with food.

The two primary objectives of my cuisine have always been flavor and purity. I have also found that because I typically work with the best seasonal, usually organic products, I inevitably end up creating dishes that are inherently healthy as well. But I had never approached cuisine from a wholly nutritional perspective until I was asked by One&Only Palmilla to put together a spa cuisine menu.

I was eager to pursue the challenge. And now, by marrying my longstanding culinary philosophy with the work of Mary Abbott Hess, one the country's foremost nutritional experts, I have originated a cuisine that is both classic Charlie Trotter and remarkably healthy.

The journey of taking my style of cuisine, which is already light and healthful because it calls for virtually no cream, butter, or heavy sauces, and reinventing it to make it even more healthful has been highly rewarding. The result is dishes that nourish both the body and soul.

The guests at One&Only Palmilla are often surprised when they try menu items that have been designated "spa cuisine." The flavors, combinations, and overall taste of these dishes are extraordinary, so that diners never have the feeling that they are surrendering exquisite food flavor in the interest of nutrition. An example of just one guest's comment illustrates this point: "If I had not been told it was spa cuisine, I wouldn't have known it—for me it was just amazing food."

That's my goal: to create cuisine that speaks to the soul of every guest because a great meal becomes a lifetime memory. I hope that the recipes in this book speak to you the way they have to so many visitors of One&Only Palmilla—that they nurture your body and renew your spirit.

CHARLIE TROTTER

Many people ask if wine has a place in a spa cuisine program. If you enjoy drinking wine, the answer is definitely yes.

Wine consumed in moderation has been proven to offer some health benefits. However, when thinking about wine as part of an overall spa cuisine regimen, you need to focus on what you like, rather than follow universally applied rigid recommendations. Our approach to spa cuisine is all about choice, and the same is true for wine. Of course, any time you consume wine, you must do so in moderation. In the same way that eating too much is not a good idea, drinking too much wine is equally irresponsible.

The experience of drinking wine is one of discovery, and just as you do when you enter a new relationship, you should undertake it slowly, and savor every step of the journey. Wine offers a sensual, complex flavor opportunity to complement foods of all kinds. And while you will not find a specific wine recommendation alongside each recipe in this book, every dish that appears is wine-friendly. The recipes have been created with *flavor* as their primary focus, and all of them can be paired effortlessly with wine.

How do you go about choosing a wine for a specific dish? You must first identify the main flavors of the dish, and then find a wine that will balance those flavors. Each recipe has been developed in a light style that coaxes out subtle tastes and plays up key ingredients. The most important thing to remember is to avoid masking those flavors and textures by selecting a wine that is too big, too bold, or too full-bodied.

Sparkling wines will pair well with the lightest seafood preparations in this book. When you are considering dishes that generally partner well with white wines, try pouring a Riesling, one of the most food-friendly wine styles. If you venture into the world of red wines, look to different styles of Pinot Noir, which have the body to stand up to some of the meat preparations while not overpowering their delicate flavors. All three of these wine styles tend to be light yet still have the level of acid necessary for successful food pairing. When serving a dessert, never choose a wine that is sweeter than the dessert itself. Remember, wine and food should balance each other, not wash each other out.

In the end, matching wines with spa cuisine follows the same rules as pairing wines with any food. Experiment until you find a match that you enjoy, and then always remember that match.

ROCHELLE SMITH
CULINARY CONSULTANT, CHARLIE TROTTER'S
AND RESTAURANT C

Morning

COCONUT, LEMONGRASS,
AND PINEAPPLE SMOOTHIE

SERVES 4

2 cups chopped Maui pineapple
1 cup nonfat plain yogurt
½ cup coconut water
1 tablespoon freshly squeezed lime juice
1-inch piece lemongrass stalk, from
*   bulb portion, grated*
2 cups crushed ice

METHOD

Combine the pineapple, yogurt, coconut water, lime juice, lemongrass,
and ice in a high-speed blender and process until smooth. Pour the smoothie
into chilled glasses.

PEACH LEMONADE

SERVES 4

4 cups water
2 cups fresh peach juice
½ cup freshly squeezed lemon juice
1 tablespoon freshly squeezed lime juice
Pinch of sugar

METHOD

Combine the water, peach juice, lemon juice, lime juice, and sugar in
a high-speed blender and process until frothy. Pour the lemonade into
ice-filled glasses.

ASIAN PEAR, PRICKLY PEAR, AND
KAFFIR LIME INFUSION

SERVES 4

1 cup peeled, chopped Asian pear
1 cup chopped prickly pear pulp
2 cups unsweetened apple juice
2 kaffir lime leaves
1 cup crushed ice

METHOD

Combine the Asian pear, prickly pear, apple juice, kaffir lime leaves, and ice in a high-speed blender and process until smooth. Pour the infusion into chilled glasses.

HEIRLOOM TOMATO AND
BASIL WATER

SERVES 4

24 Roma tomatoes, coarsely chopped
8 fresh basil leaves
Kosher salt
4 lime wedges (optional)

METHOD

Working in batches, combine the tomatoes, basil, and 1 teaspoon salt in a food processor and process until smooth. Line a large colander with cheesecloth, allowing it to overhang the sides, and place the colander over a bowl. Pour the purée into the colander and gather together the cheesecloth ends and tie them, creating a pouch. Refrigerate for 8 hours, or until all the juices from the puréed tomatoes have dripped into the bowl. Discard the solids and pour the liquid into ice-filled glasses. Garnish each glass with a lime wedge, if desired.

CUCUMBER AND MINT SMOOTHIE

SERVES 4

2 cups peeled, seeded, and chopped cucumber
¾ cup nonfat plain yogurt
¼ cup Simple Syrup (see page 213)
7 fresh mint leaves
1½ cups crushed ice

METHOD

Combine the cucumber, yogurt, Simple Syrup, mint leaves, and ice in a high-speed blender and process until smooth. Pour the smoothie into chilled glasses.

MANGO AND KAFFIR LIME LEAF
SMOOTHIE

SERVES 4

2 cups chopped mango
¼ cup chopped banana
¾ cup nonfat plain yogurt
1 kaffir lime leaf
1½ cups crushed ice

METHOD

Combine the mango, banana, yogurt, kaffir lime leaf, and ice in a high-speed blender and process until smooth. Pour the smoothie into chilled glasses.

CHOCOLATE, BANANA,
AND YOGURT SMOOTHIE

SERVES 4

2 cups chopped banana
2 cups nonfat plain yogurt
3 tablespoons cocoa powder
2 cups crushed ice

METHOD

Combine the banana, yogurt, cocoa powder, and ice in a high-speed blender and process until smooth. Pour the smoothie into chilled glasses.

CUCUMBER, MINT, APPLE,
AND KEY LIME JUICE

SERVES 4

3 English cucumbers, cut in half lengthwise
2 Granny Smith apples, chopped
2 celery stalks
3 sprigs mint
Juice of 8 Key limes

METHOD

Put the cucumbers, apples, celery, and mint through a juicer, then stir in the lime juice. Pour into chilled glasses.

EGG WHITE OMELET WITH
COLD-SMOKED STURGEON AND STEWED RADISHES

The lightly smoked sturgeon gives substance to this otherwise delicate omelet.

The addition of finely grated lemon zest and chopped chives at the end delivers a much-appreciated zing

that rounds out the flavors in the vegetables and egg whites.

SERVES 4

FOR THE VEGETABLES:

4 radishes, julienned
½ cup thinly sliced cremini mushroom
4 asparagus spears, blanched and cut into
   bite-sized pieces
2 scallions, chopped
½ teaspoon olive oil
1 tablespoon freshly squeezed lemon juice
Kosher salt and freshly ground pepper

FOR THE OMELETS:

12 egg whites
Kosher salt and freshly ground black pepper
Nonstick cooking spray
2 teaspoons clarified butter

4 ounces cold-smoked sturgeon, coarsely shredded
2 tablespoons chopped fresh chives
1 teaspoon finely grated lemon zest

METHOD

To prepare the vegetables: Heat a small sauté pan over medium heat and add the radish, mushroom, asparagus, scallions, olive oil, and lemon juice. Cook, stirring occasionally, for 2 to 3 minutes, or until the vegetables are hot. Remove from the heat, and season to taste with salt and pepper.

To prepare the omelets: Place the egg whites in a bowl and froth with a whisk. Season with ½ teaspoon salt and lightly with pepper. Lightly spray a nonstick omelet pan with nonstick cooking spray, add ½ teaspoon of the clarified butter, and place the pan over medium-high heat. Pour one-fourth of the egg whites into the hot pan and cook for about 3 minutes, or until the egg white is firm but not golden brown. Shake the omelet out of the pan onto a serving plate. Repeat until you have 4 omelets total.

ASSEMBLY

Place some of the smoked sturgeon down the middle of each omelet. Spoon the warm vegetables over the sturgeon, and sprinkle with the chives and lemon zest.

WARM MISO SOUP WITH SILKEN TOFU, SOFT POACHED EGG, AND GLASS NOODLES

As you gently touch the rich, silky egg yolk with your spoon, it breaks

and then slowly spreads into the warm miso broth.

This sensual preparation of egg, miso, and noodles is immensely satisfying.

SERVES 6

FOR THE SOUP:

½ teaspoon toasted sesame oil

2 scallions, finely minced

1 teaspoon minced fresh ginger

4 cups water

1½ teaspoons rice vinegar

3 tablespoons yellow miso

4 ounces firm silken tofu, cut into ½-inch cubes

3 shiitake mushrooms, stems removed and
    thinly sliced

FOR THE POACHED EGGS:

2 teaspoons white wine vinegar

6 eggs

4 ounces glass noodles, cooked (about 2½ cups)

METHOD

To prepare the soup: Heat the sesame oil in a saucepan over medium-high heat. Add the scallions and ginger and cook, stirring frequently, for about 30 seconds, or until the scallions are wilted and the ginger is aromatic. Add 3½ cups of the water and the rice vinegar. Whisk the miso in the remaining ½ cup water and add to the pan. Bring to a gentle simmer, add the tofu and mushrooms, and continue to cook gently just until the tofu is warm.

To prepare the eggs: Bring a wide, shallow saucepan of water to a simmer and add the wine vinegar. Working quickly, crack each egg into a small cup and add to the simmering water one at a time. Poach for 1 minute and 20 seconds, or until the whites are just set and the yolks are still soft. Remove from the water with a slotted spoon.

ASSEMBLY

Arrange some of the glass noodles in each bowl. Ladle in the soup and top with a warm poached egg.

WHOLE-WHEAT PANCAKES WITH
MAUI ONION MARMALADE AND STEWED STRAWBERRIES

Not only is this dish a great morning meal, but it can also be easily converted to an evening canapé.
Try making silver dollar–sized pancakes, topping them with the tart onion marmalade, and then garnishing with
the thyme leaves and a delicate strawberry. The maple syrup won't be missed!

SERVES 5

FOR THE PANCAKES:
1¼ cups whole-wheat flour
2¼ teaspoons baking powder
¼ teaspoon kosher salt
1 egg
1¼ cups skim milk
Nonstick cooking spray

FOR THE STRAWBERRIES:
10 strawberries, stems removed and
*   cut into small wedges*
1 teaspoon fresh thyme leaves
5 tablespoons maple syrup
2 tablespoons water

Maui Onion Marmalade (see page 209)
2 teaspoons Basil Oil (optional; see page 206)
¼ cup loosely packed micro herbs

METHOD

To prepare the pancakes: Combine the flour, baking powder, and salt in a bowl. Beat together the egg and milk in a separate bowl, then stir the egg mixture into the flour mixture to form a lumpy batter. Spray a large nonstick skillet with cooking spray and heat over medium heat. Drop the batter by spoonfuls into the hot pan, making 4-inch pancakes. Reduce the heat to low and cook for 2 to 3 minutes, or until bubbles begin to form on the cakes. Turn and cook on other side for about 1 minute, or until golden brown. You should have 15 pancakes total.

To prepare the strawberries: Place the strawberries, thyme, maple syrup, and water in a saucepan and warm gently over medium-low heat.

ASSEMBLY

Spoon some of the Maui Onion Marmalade and warm strawberries in the center of each plate and top with a pancake. Continue to layer the marmalade and strawberries between the pancakes until you have a stack 3 pancakes high, ending with strawberries and marmalade. Spoon any juices that remain in the saucepan from the strawberries around the plate. Drizzle with the Basil Oil, if desired. Sprinkle the micro herbs over the pancake stack.

TROPICAL FRUITS WITH LAVENDER-MINT YOGURT AND TOASTED ALMONDS

Here is a delightful way to start your day. The beautifully ripened fruits are brought together with a hint of lime juice and mint. The delicate lavender flavors the yogurt with just a light touch of the calming herb.

SERVES 4

FOR THE YOGURT:

1 teaspoon ground fresh lavender flowers
1 teaspoon chopped fresh mint
3 cups nonfat plain yogurt
2 tablespoons honey

FOR THE FRUITS:

1 cup thinly sliced Golden kiwifruit
1 cup thinly sliced mango
1 cup ¼-inch-thick bite-sized pineapple pieces
1 cup angle-cut papaya chunks
2 teaspoons freshly squeezed lime juice
2 teaspoons chopped fresh mint

¼ cup whole natural almonds, toasted

METHOD

To prepare the yogurt: Set aside a pinch each of the lavender and mint to use for garnish. Combine the yogurt, honey, and the remaining lavender and mint in a bowl and stir to mix.

To prepare the fruits: Place the kiwifruit, mango, pineapple, papaya, lime juice, and mint in a bowl. Toss together just until combined, being careful not to break up the fruit.

ASSEMBLY

Arrange the fruits on the diagonal on each plate, spooning any juices that remain in the bowl on top. Scatter the almonds over the fruits, and serve the yogurt in a small bowl alongside. Sprinkle the reserved lavender and mint over both the yogurt and the fruits.

SOFT POACHED EGG WITH CURED SALMON, BABY SPINACH, AND AN OLIVE OIL AND LEMON ZEST VINAIGRETTE

I have been known to enjoy this dish for lunch as well as breakfast.

Make it and you will discover that a perfectly poached egg alongside small, tender spinach leaves and smoked salmon

is an unparalleled treat. The potatoes and lemon zest are auspicious additions.

SERVES 4

FOR THE VINAIGRETTE AND VEGETABLES:

1 tablespoon minced red onion
1½ teaspoons finely grated Meyer lemon zest
1 tablespoon freshly squeezed Meyer lemon juice
1 tablespoon olive oil
Kosher salt and freshly ground black pepper
4 fingerling potatoes, cooked and sliced into bite-sized pieces
2 cups baby spinach leaves
¾ cup shaved fennel

FOR THE POACHED EGGS:

2 teaspoons white wine vinegar
4 eggs

8 paper-thin slices cold-smoked salmon (about 3 ounces total)
Freshly ground black pepper

METHOD

To prepare the vinaigrette and vegetables: Whisk together the onion, lemon zest, lemon juice, and olive oil in a small bowl and season to taste with salt and pepper. In a separate bowl, toss together the potatoes, spinach, and fennel. Add the vinaigrette to the potato mixture, toss to mix, taste, and adjust the seasoning with salt and pepper.

To prepare the eggs: Bring a wide, shallow saucepan of water to a simmer and add the vinegar. Working quickly, crack each egg into a small cup and add to the simmering water one at a time. Poach for 1 minute and 20 seconds, or until the whites are just set and the yolks are still soft. Remove from the water with a slotted spoon.

ASSEMBLY

Loosely roll 2 salmon slices and place on each plate. Arrange the spinach mixture over the salmon. Place a warm poached egg over the spinach and top with pepper. Spoon any juices that remain in the bowl from the spinach and fennel around the plate.

Midday

WARM CRAB SALAD WITH SHELLFISH BROTH
AND SOY-BRAISED DAIKON RADISH

The sweet crabmeat melds with the perfectly balanced shellfish-infused broth, while the soy-braised daikon pieces

are like small hidden treasures, waiting to be discovered. If you are unable to find the yuzu juice

(which shines brightly in the broth), use equal parts freshly squeezed lemon, lime, and grapefruit juice in its place.

SERVES 4

FOR THE CRAB SALAD:

12 ounces crabmeat, picked over for shell fragments
2 tablespoons freshly squeezed lime juice
2 tablespoons low-fat mayonnaise
2 tablespoons minced red bell pepper
1 tablespoon minced shallot
1 tablespoon minced jalapeño chile
1 tablespoon chopped fresh chives
1 tablespoon chopped fresh flat-leaf parsley
Kosher salt and freshly ground black pepper

FOR THE DAIKON AND BROTH:

1 cup peeled, medium-diced daikon
1 tablespoon reduced-sodium soy sauce
1 tablespoon mirin
1 tablespoon yuzu juice
2 teaspoons rice vinegar
¼ cup water
3 cups Shellfish Stock (see page 212)
1 tablespoon coarsely chopped fresh cilantro

Freshly ground black pepper
4 teaspoons assorted fresh micro herbs

METHOD

To prepare the crab salad: Preheat the oven to 350 degrees. Line a sheet pan with parchment paper, and place 4 ring molds, each 3 inches in diameter and 1 inch deep, on the pan. In a bowl, combine the crabmeat, lime juice, mayonnaise, bell pepper, shallot, chile, chives, parsley, and ¼ teaspoon each salt and pepper and stir to mix. Fill the ring molds with the crab salad. Place in the oven for 10 minutes, or just until warm.

To prepare the daikon and broth: Place the daikon, soy sauce, mirin, yuzu juice, vinegar, and water in a saucepan. Bring to a simmer and cook for about 5 minutes, or until the daikon is just tender. Add the stock and cilantro and heat until hot.

ASSEMBLY

Place a warm crab salad in the center of each bowl, and carefully remove the ring mold. Ladle the broth and daikon mixture around the crab salad, and top with pepper. Sprinkle 1 teaspoon micro herbs over each salad.

MUSHROOM BROTH WITH
STEAMED GINGERED-MUSHROOM WONTONS

This recipe delivers a light and delicate dish, but you can easily double

the amount of mushroom wontons to create a more substantial portion. Whenever I sit down to this preparation,

I look forward to enjoying a toothsome wonton in every spoonful.

SERVES 4

FOR THE WONTONS:
2 tablespoons minced fresh ginger
2 teaspoons minced garlic
1 teaspoon olive oil
¼ cup chopped scallion
1 cup Roasted Mushrooms, chopped (see page 212)
Kosher salt and freshly ground black pepper
16 round wonton skins, 2½ inches in diameter

4 cups Mushroom Broth, hot (see page 209)

FOR THE GARNISH:
½ cup diced water chestnut
2 radishes, thinly sliced
¼ cup finely chopped scallion
1 cup finely chopped bok choy, green part only
1¼ teaspoons toasted sesame oil
½ lime

METHOD

To prepare the wontons: Place the ginger, garlic, and olive oil in a sauté pan over low heat and sweat for about 2 minutes, or until the garlic is translucent. Add the scallion and Roasted Mushrooms, stir to combine, and season to taste with salt and pepper. Remove from the heat and let cool to room temperature. Lay the wonton skins on a dry work surface. Put about 1 tablespoon of the mushroom mixture in the center of each wonton skin. Lightly brush the edge of each wonton skin with water, fold over to create a half-moon, and gently press the edges together to seal. Then bring together the 2 outer points, and seal them together with a damp finger. Arrange the wontons on the bottom of a bamboo steamer basket, and place the basket over a pan of simmering water. Cover and steam for about 4 minutes, or until the wonton skins are translucent.

ASSEMBLY

Place 4 wontons in each bowl and ladle in the broth. Garnish with the water chestnut, radishes, scallion, bok choy, and sesame oil. Squeeze the juice from the lime half over the bowls just before serving.

YELLOW TOMATO SOUP WITH ROASTED CAULIFLOWER AND BROCCOFLOWER AND CUMIN-SEED VINAIGRETTE

I like to offer this soup near the end of tomato season, when the nights begin to cool.

It isn't served piping hot but just warmed through. If you would like to accompany it with something crunchy,

crisp garlic-Parmesan crostini would be excellent for dipping into the bowl.

SERVES 4

FOR THE SOUP:

1½ red onions, cut into small dice
2 cloves garlic, chopped
2 teaspoons olive oil
4 large yellow tomatoes, peeled, seeded,
   and chopped
¼ cup water
1 tablespoon balsamic vinegar
Kosher salt and freshly ground black pepper

FOR THE CAULIFLOWER AND
BROCCOFLOWER:

12 slices cauliflower, 2 inches wide and ¼ inch thick
12 slices broccoflower, 1 inch wide and ¼ inch thick
1 teaspoon olive oil
Kosher salt and freshly ground black pepper
1 tablespoon chopped fresh flat-leaf parsley

FOR THE CUMIN-SEED VINAIGRETTE:

1 teaspoon cumin seeds, toasted and crushed
1 teaspoon red wine vinegar
1 tablespoon chopped fresh chives
1 tablespoon olive oil
Kosher salt and freshly ground black pepper

1 cup loosely packed frisée leaves
2 teaspoons Basil Oil (optional; see page 206)
Freshly ground black pepper

METHOD

To prepare the soup: Place the onions, garlic, and olive oil in a large sauté pan and sweat over medium-low heat for about 5 minutes, or until the onions are translucent. Add the tomatoes and cook, stirring occasionally, for 10 minutes, or until the tomatoes begin to dry out. Add the water and balsamic vinegar and continue to cook for 10 minutes longer to blend the flavors. Transfer to a blender and process until a thick, souplike consistency forms. If necessary, add a little more water to achieve the correct consistency. Season with ¼ teaspoon each salt and pepper, then reheat if necessary.

To prepare the cauliflower and broccoflower: Preheat the oven to 325 degrees. Toss the cauliflower and broccoflower with the olive oil and season with ⅛ teaspoon each salt and pepper. Place in a single layer in a baking dish and roast for 30 to 40 minutes, or until light golden brown and tender. Remove from the oven and sprinkle with the parsley.

To prepare the Cumin-Seed Vinaigrette: Whisk together the cumin, red wine vinegar, and chives in a small bowl. Whisk in the olive oil and ⅛ teaspoon each salt and pepper.

ASSEMBLY

Pour some of the warm soup into the bottom of each shallow bowl. Arrange some of the cauliflower and broccoflower slices on top of the soup. Sprinkle the frisée over the soup, and then drizzle with the Cumin-Seed Vinaigrette and finally with the Basil Oil, if desired. Top with pepper.

SALAD OF PEACHES WITH RADISHES, PEPPER CRESS, AND ROASTED RED ONION

Roasting the peaches concentrates their natural sweetness. At the same time, the sharpness

of the pepper cress and the tartness of the plums deliver a welcome contrast to the peaches' sweetness. The addition

of a piece of lightly grilled fish would turn this salad into a light dinner main course.

SERVES 4

4 white or yellow peaches, peeled and pitted
1 small red onion, thinly sliced
2 tablespoons balsamic vinegar
3 tablespoons olive oil
Kosher salt and freshly ground black pepper
¼ cup water
2 teaspoons rice vinegar
3 Mariposa plums, peeled, pitted, and thinly sliced
2 white radishes, thinly sliced
2 pink radishes, thinly sliced
2 purple radishes, thinly sliced
4 cups loosely packed pepper cress
1½ teaspoons freshly squeezed lemon juice

METHOD

To prepare the peaches: Preheat the oven to 200 degrees. Slice 3 of the peaches into ½-inch-thick wedges; reserve the remaining peach. Place the wedges on a nonstick sheet pan and bake for 40 minutes. Flip the wedges over and continue to bake for 30 to 40 minutes, or until the wedges are a light golden brown. Remove from the oven.

To prepare the onion: Increase the oven temperature to 375 degrees. Toss together the red onion, balsamic vinegar, and 2 teaspoons of the olive oil in a small bowl. Season lightly with salt and pepper and transfer to a small baking dish. Bake for 20 to 25 minutes, or until all of the balsamic vinegar has been absorbed by the onion. Remove from the oven and let cool completely.

To prepare the vinaigrette: Coarsely chop the reserved peach and place in a blender. Add the water, process until smooth, and then strain through a fine-mesh sieve into a small bowl. Slowly whisk in the remaining 2 tablespoons plus 1 teaspoon olive oil and the rice vinegar, and season to taste with salt and pepper.

To prepare the salad: Place the plums, radishes, baked peaches, pepper cress, and red onion mixture in a bowl. Drizzle with 3 tablespoons of the vinaigrette and the lemon juice and toss gently. Season with ¼ teaspoon each salt and pepper and toss again.

ASSEMBLY

Arrange some of the salad in the center of each plate and spoon some of the remaining vinaigrette around it. Top with pepper.

STEAMED CHICKEN WITH PRESERVED CARROTS, PEPPERS, AND DAIKON WITH MARINE CIDER VINAIGRETTE

A perfectly steamed chicken breast is hard to beat. Here, I have coupled it with crisp vegetables
flavored with marine cider vinaigrette and a touch of Thai fish sauce. If you are unable to find marine-flavored cider vinegar
(cider vinegar seasoned with marine herbs and sea salt), any good-quality apple cider vinegar may be used.

SERVES 4

FOR THE MARINE CIDER
VINAIGRETTE:
1 tablespoon olive oil
2 teaspoons marine-flavored cider vinegar
2 teaspoons chopped fresh cilantro
2 tablespoons thinly sliced scallion
Mineral salt

FOR THE CHICKEN:
1 tablespoon minced fresh ginger
2 cloves garlic, finely chopped
2 tablespoons finely chopped lemongrass,
   from bulb portion
2 boneless, skinless chicken breast halves
Kosher salt and freshly ground black pepper

FOR THE VEGETABLES:
1 cup peeled, julienned carrot, steamed
1 red bell pepper, seeded and julienned
½ cup peeled, julienned daikon
2 tablespoons chopped fresh cilantro
1 teaspoon black sesame seeds
1 teaspoon white sesame seeds
2 tablespoons freshly squeezed lime juice
2 teaspoons Thai fish sauce
2 teaspoons toasted sesame oil
Kosher salt and freshly ground black pepper

FOR THE RED BELL PEPPER PURÉE
2 tablespoons chopped roasted red bell pepper
2 tablespoons water
Kosher salt

METHOD

To prepare the Marine Cider Vinaigrette: Combine the olive oil, vinegar, cilantro, scallion, and ½ teaspoon mineral salt in a small bowl and whisk together.

To prepare the chicken: Combine the ginger, garlic, and lemongrass in a small bowl. Season the chicken with ¼ teaspoon each salt and pepper and then rub the chicken with the ginger mixture. Place the chicken breasts on the bottom of a bamboo steamer basket, and place the basket over a pan of simmering water. Cover and steam for 12 to 15 minutes, or until the chicken is just cooked. Thinly slice the chicken and toss with the vinaigrette.

To prepare the vegetables: Combine the carrot, bell pepper, daikon, cilantro, and black and white sesame seeds in a bowl and toss to mix. In a separate bowl, whisk together the lime juice, fish sauce, and sesame oil. Add the lime juice mixture to the vegetables and toss to mix. Season with ¼ teaspoon each salt and pepper and toss again.

To prepare the red bell pepper purée: Combine the roasted bell pepper and water in a blender and process until smooth. Pass through a fine-mesh sieve into a bowl and season lightly with salt.

ASSEMBLY

Mound some of the vegetable mixture in the center of each plate, top with some of the chicken mixture, and then more of the vegetable mixture. Drizzle any juices from both mixtures around the plate, and spoon some of the pepper purée around the plate.

SEA SCALLOPS WITH FRESH SOYBEANS
AND GINGER-SOY-HIJIKI BROTH

The broth in this dish explodes with complex flavors imparted by the seaweed, soy, mirin, and ginger.

The buttery scallops take on just enough of the ginger and soy sauce to complement their meaty flesh. I enjoy this broth

so much that I have puréed it with tofu for extra body and then used it as a sauce or purée.

SERVES 4

GINGER-SOY-HIJIKI BROTH
¼ cup dried hijiki seaweed
2 cups water
1 tablespoon finely diced jalapeño chile
1 tablespoon finely diced shallot
1 tablespoon minced fresh ginger
1 teaspoon minced garlic
2 tablespoons rice vinegar
1 tablespoon mirin
2 tablespoons reduced-sodium soy sauce

FOR THE SCALLOPS:
4 large sea scallops, muscle trimmed
Kosher salt and freshly ground black pepper
1 teaspoon grapeseed oil
1 tablespoon freshly squeezed lemon juice
1 teaspoon sesame seeds, toasted
1 tablespoon fresh cilantro chiffonade

FOR THE GARNISH:
½ cup shelled fresh soybeans (edamame), blanched
¾ cup diced firm silken tofu
4 water chestnuts, thinly sliced
4 teaspoons fresh flat-leaf parsley leaves
4 teaspoons Preserved Ginger (see page 209)

METHOD

To prepare the broth: Soak the hijiki in cold water to cover for 30 minutes, then drain. Place the drained hijiki, water, chile, shallot, ginger, garlic, vinegar, mirin, and soy sauce in a saucepan and simmer for 15 minutes.

To prepare the scallops: Lightly season the scallops with salt and pepper. Preheat a sauté pan with the grapeseed oil over high heat. Add the scallops and cook, turning once, for 1½ minutes on each side, or until slightly underdone. Add the lemon juice, sesame seeds, and cilantro and cook, spooning the mixture over the scallops and turning them once, for 1 minute longer, or until the scallops are coated with the mixture.

ASSEMBLY

Place some of the soybeans, tofu, water chestnuts, and parsley, in each bowl. Place a scallop in the center of each bowl, and sprinkle with the Preserved Ginger. Ladle in ½ cup of the broth.

GRILLED ASPARAGUS, HEARTS OF PALM, AND SHIITAKE MUSHROOMS WITH MARCONA ALMONDS AND MANCHEGO CHEESE

The finely grated Manchego cheese encases the vegetables like a delicate dusting of fresh snow,

while the vinaigrette coats the meaty vegetables with just enough tartness to awaken your senses. When I enjoy this dish,

I like to make sure I get a little bit of each component in every bite.

SERVES 4

FOR THE VINAIGRETTE:
2 tablespoons freshly squeezed lemon juice
2 tablespoons freshly squeezed orange juice
1 teaspoon reduced-sodium soy sauce
1 tablespoon olive oil
1 teaspoon Dijon mustard
Kosher salt and freshly ground black pepper

FOR THE VEGETABLES:
16 green asparagus spears, trimmed and grilled
16 white asparagus spears, trimmed and grilled
16 shiitake mushrooms, stems removed and grilled
4 hearts of palm stalks, sliced on the diagonal
16 small basil leaves

FOR THE GARNISH:
¼ cup blanched Marcona almonds, toasted
2 ounces Manchego or Parmesan cheese, finely grated
Freshly ground black pepper

METHOD

To prepare the vinaigrette: Combine the lemon juice, orange juice, soy sauce, olive oil, and mustard in a small bowl and whisk together. Season to taste with salt and pepper.

To prepare the vegetables: Cut the asparagus into 2-inch lengths and place in a bowl. Cut the mushrooms into thick slices and add to the asparagus. Add the hearts of palm, basil leaves, and vinaigrette and toss to mix.

ASSEMBLY

Place some of the asparagus mixture in the center of each plate. Sprinkle with the basil, almonds, and cheese. Top with pepper. Spoon any juices from the bowl that held the vegetables around the plate.

SOBA NOODLES WITH HIJIKI SEAWEED, WATER CHESTNUTS, AND RED MISO BROTH

The broth for this Asian-inspired dish displays an ideal balance of flavors and textures
that blend yet never fully lose their distinctiveness. The nuances of hijiki seaweed, garlic, ginger,
and red miso can be detected in every spoonful.

SERVES 4

FOR THE NOODLES:

6 ounces dried soba noodles, cooked (4 cups)
    and warm

2 tablespoons dried hijiki seaweed, soaked in cold
    water to cover for 30 minutes and drained

2 teaspoons toasted sesame oil

1½ teaspoons reduced-sodium soy sauce

1 tablespoon yuzu juice

1 tablespoon chopped fresh flat-leaf parsley

½ cup julienned Roasted Mushrooms,
    shiitake only, warm (see page 212)

1 teaspoon rice vinegar

1 tablespoon hoisin sauce

FOR THE BROTH:

6 cups Chicken Stock or Vegetable Stock
    (see page 207 or 213)

1½ tablespoons reduced-sodium soy sauce

2 teaspoons minced fresh ginger

1 teaspoon minced garlic

1 tablespoon yuzu juice

1 tablespoon mirin

3 tablespoons red miso

2 tablespoons thinly sliced scallion

12 baby bok choy leaves, trimmed

Kosher salt and freshly ground black pepper

FOR THE GARNISH:

½ cup small-diced water chestnut

½ cup sliced bamboo shoot, julienned

1 red bell pepper, seeded and julienned

METHOD

To prepare the noodles: Combine the warm noodles, hijiki seaweed, sesame oil, soy sauce, yuzu juice, parsley, Roasted Mushrooms, vinegar, and hoisin sauce in a bowl and toss together until thoroughly combined.

To prepare the broth: Place the stock, soy sauce, ginger, garlic, and yuzu juice in a saucepan and bring to a gentle simmer. Scoop out about ½ cup of the hot broth, whisk the miso into it, and then add to the pan. Add the scallion and bok choy and simmer gently just until the bok choy wilts. Do not allow to boil. Remove from the heat and season to taste with salt and pepper.

ASSEMBLY

Twist some of the noodles into a mound and place in the center of each bowl. Sprinkle the water chestnut, bamboo shoot, and bell pepper around the bowl, and ladle in the hot broth.

COLD-POACHED SALMON
WITH HEARTS OF PALM AND TAMARIND

Cold poaching the fish ensures that it will be moist and delicate. It also transforms

the court bouillon you use for the poaching liquid into a nicely flavored fish stock that can be used for another recipe.

You may opt to cook the salmon by another method, too, such as slow roasting or sous vide.

SERVES 4

FOR THE SALMON:

4 4-ounce salmon fillets, skin removed
Kosher salt and freshly ground black pepper
3 cups Court Bouillon, simmering (see page 208)
2 teaspoons finely grated lemon zest
1 tablespoon finely chopped fresh chives

FOR THE SALAD:

2 cups thinly sliced hearts of palm
1 cup orange segments
6 tablespoons tamarind juice (paste thinned
    with water)
2 teaspoons freshly squeezed lime juice
1 tablespoon olive oil
Kosher salt and freshly ground black pepper
4 cups loosely packed mâche

METHOD

To prepare the salmon: Season the salmon with ⅛ teaspoon each salt and pepper and place in a small baking dish. Pour the simmering Court Bouillon over the salmon and cover. Allow the salmon to cook slowly in the hot liquid for 5 minutes, then turn the salmon over and allow it to sit in the hot liquid for about 5 minutes longer, or until cooked medium. Carefully remove the salmon from the liquid, season the salmon lightly with salt and pepper, and sprinkle with the lemon zest and chives. Let cool to room temperature. The Court Bouillon may be reserved for another use or discarded.

To prepare the salad: Combine the hearts of palm, orange segments, 2 tablespoons of the tamarind juice, the lime juice, and the olive oil in a bowl and toss to mix. Season with ⅛ teaspoon each salt and pepper and toss again. Fold in the mâche just before serving.

ASSEMBLY

Drizzle 1 tablespoon of the remaining tamarind juice in a random pattern on each plate. Arrange a bed of the salad in the center of each plate and top with a piece of salmon.

GRILLED PRAWNS WITH
CURRIED CUCUMBER-YOGURT SAUCE

The cucumber-yogurt sauce could almost be a stand-alone side dish.

If you want to eat this preparation while you are on the go, toss the prawns with the cucumber-yogurt sauce

and spoon the mix into whole-wheat pita bread. Who says you can't eat healthy on the go!

SERVES 4

FOR THE PRAWNS:

*20 prawns, peeled and deveined,
    with tail segments intact*
2 tablespoons olive oil
2 tablespoons minced fresh ginger
4 cloves garlic, minced
2 teaspoons finely grated lemon zest
2 teaspoons finely grated lime zest
1 tablespoon chopped fresh cilantro
Kosher salt and freshly ground black pepper
½ lime

FOR THE CURRIED
CUCUMBER-YOGURT SAUCE:

¾ cup nonfat plain yogurt
2 tablespoons freshly squeezed lime juice
3 tablespoons yellow curry paste
1 tablespoon chopped fresh cilantro
*¾ English cucumber, peeled, cut in half
    lengthwise, seeds discarded, and sliced
    crosswise ¼ inch thick*
Kosher salt and freshly ground black pepper

4 teaspoons fresh cilantro leaves

METHOD

To prepare the prawns: Place the prawns, olive oil, ginger, garlic, lemon zest, lime zest, and cilantro in a resealable plastic bag. Seal the bag closed and marinate the prawns in the refrigerator for at least 1 hour or for up to overnight. Soak 4 bamboo skewers in water to cover for at least 30 minutes. Remove the prawns from the marinade and discard the marinade. Drain the skewers and thread 5 prawns on each skewer. Season the prawns with ¼ teaspoon each salt and pepper. Grill the skewers over a medium-hot fire for 2 to 3 minutes on the first side, or until the shrimp color. Turn the skewers and continue grilling for 1 to 2 minutes longer, or until the shrimp are opaque throughout. Remove the skewers from the grill and squeeze the juice from the lime half over the prawns. Remove the prawns from the skewers just before serving.

To prepare the Curried Cucumber-Yogurt Sauce: Combine the yogurt, lime juice, curry paste, and chopped cilantro in a bowl and whisk until smooth. Fold in the cucumber and season to taste with salt and pepper.

ASSEMBLY

Spoon the Curried Cucumber-Yogurt Sauce in a zigzag on each plate and top with 5 prawns. Sprinkle 1 teaspoon cilantro leaves around each plate.

STEAMED CABRILLA WITH SPAGHETTI SQUASH
AND CHINESE LONG BEANS

Slender Chinese long beans can be found in most Asian markets, usually looped and tied as if a length of rope.

Here, they are tossed with traditional Asian seasonings that cling to them nicely. The firm-fleshed cabrilla stands up well

to the dominant flavors of the long beans. If you cannot find cabrilla, bass or cod will work in its place.

SERVES 4

FOR THE FISH:

4 4-ounce pieces cabrilla fillet, skin removed
Kosher salt and freshly ground black pepper
1 lemongrass stalk, chopped
6 sprigs cilantro
2 cloves garlic, smashed
4 ¼-inch-thick slices fresh ginger
1 jalapeño chile, cut in half

FOR THE SAUCE:

1 tablespoon reduced-sodium soy sauce
1 teaspoon yuzu juice
2 teaspoons olive oil
1 teaspoon Basil Oil (see page 206)
2 teaspoons finely chopped fresh chives
2 teaspoons finely chopped scallion

FOR THE BEANS:

2 teaspoons hoisin sauce
1 teaspoon toasted sesame oil
1 teaspoon chile-garlic paste
1 tablespoon yuzu juice
1 teaspoon reduced-sodium soy sauce
1½ teaspoons black sesame seeds
8 long beans, blanched and cut into 4-inch lengths

1 spaghetti squash, roasted and flesh scraped
*   and kept hot*
¼ cup loosely packed fresh micro opal basil leaves

METHOD

To prepare the fish: Season the fish with ¼ teaspoon each salt and pepper and place on the bottom of a bamboo steamer basket. Place the lemongrass, cilantro, garlic, ginger, and chile on the bottom of a second bamboo steamer basket and place this basket over a pan of simmering water. (The fragrance of these ingredients will be carried along in the steam and flavor the fish.) Top with the basket holding the fish, cover, and steam for 5 to 7 minutes, or until the fish is just opaque at the center.

To prepare the sauce: Combine the soy sauce, yuzu juice, olive oil, Basil Oil, chives, and scallion in a small bowl and whisk together.

To prepare the beans: Combine the hoisin sauce, sesame oil, chile-garlic paste, yuzu juice, soy sauce, and sesame seeds in a sauté pan and warm over medium heat. Fold in the beans. Continue to warm over medium heat until the beans are hot.

ASSEMBLY

Place some of the squash in the center of each plate and top with some of the long beans. Set a piece of the steamed fish over the beans and spoon the sauce over the fish and around the plate. Sprinkle with the opal basil.

GRILLED CHICKEN WITH QUINOA TABBOULEH
AND PARSLEY VINAIGRETTE

Quinoa, native to the Andes, is not only extremely high in nutrients, but is also a great medium for this tabbouleh.

This would be a great dish to take to the beach for a picnic: simply toss all the ingredients together and chill until ready to serve.

I have even been known to eat it right out of the to-go container before arriving at my destination!

SERVES 4

4 small boneless, skinless chicken breast halves,
*   grilled and thinly sliced*

FOR THE QUINOA:
3 cups cooked quinoa, at room temperature
*   or lightly chilled*
½ cup small-diced cucumber, skin on
¼ cup small-diced red bell pepper
2 tablespoons chopped fresh flat-leaf parsley
2 teaspoons chopped fresh mint
2 tablespoons olive oil
1 tablespoon freshly squeezed lemon juice
2 tablespoons minced red onion
1½ tablespoons sherry vinegar
Kosher salt and freshly ground black pepper

FOR THE PARSLEY VINAIGRETTE:
2 tablespoons freshly squeezed lemon juice
1½ tablespoons water
1 tablespoon olive oil
2½ tablespoons finely chopped fresh flat-leaf parsley
Kosher salt and freshly ground black pepper

METHOD

Have the grilled chicken at room temperature.

To prepare the quinoa: Combine the quinoa, cucumber, bell pepper, parsley, mint, olive oil, lemon juice, red onion, and vinegar in a large bowl and toss to mix. Season with ½ teaspoon salt and ⅛ teaspoon pepper.

To prepare the Parsley Vinaigrette: Whisk together the lemon juice and water in a small bowl. Whisk in the olive oil and then fold in the parsley. Season lightly with salt and pepper.

ASSEMBLY

Place some of the quinoa in the center of each plate and arrange the chicken over the quinoa. Spoon the Parsley Vinaigrette over the chicken and quinoa and around the plate.

WATERMELON SOUP WITH
CANTALOUPE GRANITÉ AND SPEARMINT

The best chilled melon soups are laced with aromatic flavors and are refreshing in the
summer heat, and this one delivers on both counts! The vibrant granité instantly melts in your mouth,
releasing the natural sweetness of the cantaloupe and spearmint.

SERVES 4

FOR THE GRANITÉ:
3 cups chopped cantaloupe
1½ teaspoons chopped fresh spearmint

FOR THE SOUP:
4 cups chopped red watermelon

FOR THE GARNISH:
½ cup diced red watermelon
½ cup diced cantaloupe
½ cup diced jicama
2 tablespoons freshly squeezed lime juice
1½ teaspoons chopped fresh spearmint
1 teaspoon finely grated lime zest
½ cup diced watermelon rind, outer green
   layer removed
2 teaspoons fresh tiny spearmint leaves

METHOD

To prepare the granité: In a food processor, purée the chopped cantaloupe
until it is a thick liquid. Pass it through a fine-mesh sieve placed over a bowl, and
discard the pulp. Pour the juice into a shallow pan and place in the freezer.
After 30 minutes, remove the pan from the freezer and stir the juice with a spoon.
Return the pan to the freezer for about 1 hour, or until the juice begins to harden.
Then, every 20 minutes, scrape the granité with a spoon, creating a snowlike
consistency, for 10 to 12 hours total, or until the granité is set. Sprinkle with
the chopped spearmint just before serving.

To prepare the soup: In a high-speed blender, process the chopped watermelon
until it is a medium-bodied liquid. Pass it through a fine-mesh sieve placed over
a bowl, and discard the pulp. Chill the juice well before serving.

To prepare the garnish: Place the watermelon, cantaloupe, and jicama in
separate bowls. Add 2 teaspoons of the lime juice, ½ teaspoon of the chopped
spearmint, and one-third of the lime zest to each of the melons and toss to mix.
Add the watermelon rind and the remaining 2 teaspoons lime juice, ½ teaspoon
chopped spearmint, and lime zest to the jicama and toss to mix.

ASSEMBLY

Using a ring mold 1½ inches in diameter and 2 inches deep, arrange one-fourth
each of the watermelon and cantaloupe at 2 corners of each bowl. Arrange
one-eighth of the jicama mixture in each of the 2 remaining corners in each bowl.
Place a mound of the granité on top of one of the jicama mounds. Pour the
chilled watermelon soup around the granité and fruits and sprinkle with
the spearmint leaves.

VANILLA–KAFFIR LIME–SOY MILK PANNA COTTA WITH MANGO AND RASPBERRIES

This delicate panna cotta melts in your mouth. Vanilla and mango are a classic pairing, but the addition of the kaffir lime leaf moves that traditional match to a new dimension. You may prepare this dessert year-round, substituting other fruits at the height of their season for the mango and raspberries.

SERVES 8

FOR THE PANNA COTTA:

3 sheets gelatin

1½ cups soy milk

4 ounces firm silken tofu

2 tablespoons honey

Seeds from 1 vanilla bean

1 kaffir lime leaf

Pinch of kosher salt

FOR THE MANGO AND RASPBERRIES:

½ cup brunoise-cut mango

3 tablespoons plus 2 teaspoons freshly squeezed lime juice

1 tablespoon water

½ kaffir lime leaf, cut into a fine chiffonade

Pinch of vanilla bean seeds

32 small red raspberries

32 small golden raspberries

8 teaspoons honeycomb

METHOD

To prepare the panna cotta: Soften the gelatin in cold water to cover for 5 minutes. Just before using, remove the sheets from the water and squeeze out any excess liquid. Combine the soy milk, tofu, honey, vanilla bean seeds, kaffir lime leaf, and salt in a saucepan. Bring to a simmer and simmer for 3 minutes. Remove from the heat and whisk in the softened gelatin. Let cool to room temperature, then purée in a blender until smooth. Pour into a large glass measuring pitcher and refrigerate for 1 hour, stirring every 10 to 15 minutes to ensure the vanilla seeds do not sink to the bottom of the container and to help dissolve the froth that developed in the blender. Pour the mixture into 8 nonstick fluted molds, each about 3 inches in diameter and ½ inch deep. Refrigerate for 3 hours, or until set.

To prepare the mango and the raspberries: Combine the mango, 2 tablespoons of the lime juice, the water, the kaffir lime leaf, and the vanilla bean seeds in a bowl and toss to mix. In a separate bowl, combine the raspberries and the remaining 1 tablespoon plus 2 teaspoons lime juice and toss to mix.

ASSEMBLY

Dip the bottom of each panna cotta mold in warm water for 3 to 5 seconds, invert onto the center of a plate, and carefully lift off the mold. Spoon the mango and raspberry garnishes alongside each panna cotta, then place 1 teaspoon of the honeycomb on top.

POPPY-SEED ANGEL FOOD CAKE WITH BLUEBERRIES AND LEMON ZEST

These guilt-free minicakes are almost too good to be true. I suggest that you make a double recipe,

as you will be surprised at how fast these little clouds can disappear. Here, I have prepared them bite sized,

but the same batter could be baked in an angel food cake pan and the cake cut into slices.

SERVES 6

FOR THE CAKES:
5 tablespoons cake flour
¼ cup plus 2 tablespoons sugar
3 egg whites
½ teaspoon cream of tartar
Pinch of kosher salt
1 tablespoon poppy seeds
1½ teaspoons finely grated lemon zest

FOR THE BLUEBERRIES:
1½ cups blueberries
¼ cup water
1 tablespoon finely grated lemon zest
2 teaspoons freshly squeezed lemon juice

FOR THE GARNISH:
1 tablespoon finely grated lemon zest
2 teaspoons honey (optional)
2 teaspoons fresh tiny mint leaves

METHOD

To prepare the cakes: Preheat the oven to 375 degrees. Line a sheet pan with parchment paper. Place 12 ring molds, each 2 inches in diameter and 1¾ inches deep, on the prepared pan. Sift together the cake flour and 2 tablespoons of the sugar and set aside. Using an electric mixer, whip the egg whites and cream of tartar until soft peaks form. Add the salt and then slowly add the ¼ cup sugar while continuing to whip until stiff peaks form. Fold the flour mixture into the egg whites just until combined. Fold the poppy seeds and lemon zest into the egg white mixture. Fill the ring molds three-fourths full with the batter. Bake for 12 to 15 minutes, or until light golden brown. Let cool briefly and then lift off the molds.

To prepare the blueberries: Place the blueberries, water, lemon zest, and lemon juice in a saucepan and cook over medium heat for 3 to 4 minutes, or until the berries are soft and all the flavors come together. Let cool to room temperature.

ASSEMBLY

Spoon some of the blueberries in the center of each plate, allowing the juices to run. Set 2 cakes on top of the blueberries. Sprinkle the lemon zest over the cakes and around the plate. If desired, drizzle the honey over the cakes. Sprinkle the mint leaves over the cakes and around the plates.

Evening

GRILLED JAPANESE EGGPLANT SALAD
WITH BASIL AND SCALLION

Before turning off the barbecue at the end of an evening's dinner, I usually grill some

extra vegetables for use in a salad the next day. That's how this salad came about. I like to serve it meat free,

but a piece of perfectly grilled chicken would be a delightful addition.

SERVES 4

FOR THE VEGETABLES:

3 tablespoons balsamic vinegar

2 tablespoons olive oil

3 tablespoons finely chopped fresh basil

4 Japanese eggplants, cut in half lengthwise
*   and flesh side scored*

Kosher salt and freshly ground black pepper

1 red onion, cut into ½-inch-thick rings

1 head radicchio, cut into 8 wedges

8 scallions, trimmed

¼ cup loosely packed fresh flat-leaf parsley leaves

½ cup loosely packed frisée leaves

3 ounces soft fresh goat cheese, crumbled

2 teaspoons aged balsamic vinegar

METHOD

To prepare the vegetables: Combine the balsamic vinegar, olive oil, and basil in a small bowl and whisk to make a vinaigrette. Brush the flesh side of the eggplant halves with some of the vinaigrette and season them with ⅛ teaspoon each salt and pepper. Brush the red onion rings, radicchio wedges, and scallions with some of the vinaigrette and season with ⅛ teaspoon each salt and pepper. Reserve any leftover vinaigrette for garnish. Place all of the prepared vegetables over a medium-hot fire and grill, turning as needed, until tender. The scallions and radicchio wedges will be ready in 4 to 6 minutes, while the red onions and the eggplants will take up to 10 to 12 minutes. Let the vegetables cool slightly. Cut the eggplants into large pieces on the diagonal. Cut the radicchio wedges into thirds, discarding the thick inner core. Cut the red onion rings into ½-inch pieces, and chop the scallions.

ASSEMBLY

Place the eggplant, red onion, radicchio, scallions, parsley, and frisée in a large bowl. Toss together gently and season to taste with salt and pepper. Place some of the salad in the center of each plate and sprinkle the goat cheese over the top. Drizzle the aged balsamic vinegar and any remaining vinaigrette on each plate just before serving. Top with pepper.

TERRINE OF POACHED LEEKS AND SPOT PRAWNS
WITH ROASTED APPLE–CURRY SAUCE

Layering ingredients in a terrine yields an elaborate presentation

guaranteed to impress your guests. But the components in this dish will still shine

if they are simply tossed together and presented on a serving platter.

SERVES 6

FOR THE TERRINE:
5 sheets gelatin
1 cup Shellfish Stock (see page 212)
3 leeks, white part only (6 inches long), poached
18 spot prawns, peeled, deveined, and steamed
Kosher salt and freshly ground black pepper

FOR THE ROASTED
APPLE–CURRY SAUCE:
¼ cup chopped red onion
1 teaspoon minced garlic
1 tablespoon olive oil
1 teaspoon yellow curry powder
1 cup diced, peeled apple
½ cup water
2 tablespoons nonfat plain yogurt
Kosher salt and freshly ground black pepper

FOR THE FENNEL:
1 cup thinly sliced fennel
2 teaspoons chopped fennel fronds
1 tablespoon freshly squeezed lemon juice
Kosher salt and freshly ground pepper

FOR THE GARNISH:
1 tablespoon Herb Oil (optional; see page 208)
3 tablespoons coarsely chopped orange segments
⅓ cup micro fennel sprouts
Freshly ground black pepper

METHOD

To prepare the terrine: Line a 6 by 2¼ by 1½-inch metal terrine mold with plastic wrap, allowing some plastic wrap to overhang the sides. Soften the gelatin in cold water to cover for 5 minutes. Just before using, remove the sheets from the water and squeeze out any excess liquid. Warm the stock in a saucepan and whisk in the softened gelatin until dissolved. Cut each leek in half lengthwise. Lay both halves of 1 leek, cut side down, in the bottom of the prepared terrine and arrange 6 prawns in a layer on top, spooning some of the gelatin mixture over each layer. Repeat the layers twice, ending with prawns and spooning the gelatin mixture over each layer. Cover the terrine tightly with the overhanging plastic wrap and press down firmly on the top with your hand to release the excess gelatin, filling in all the gaps. Refrigerate the terrine overnight. Remove the pins from the mold so the sides fall away, remove the terrine from the base, and rewrap the plastic wrap tightly around the terrine. Using a sharp knife, cut the terrine crosswise into 6 equal slices. Carefully remove the plastic wrap from the slices and season them lightly with salt and pepper.

To prepare the Roasted Apple–Curry Sauce: Place the onion, garlic, and olive oil in a small sauté pan and sweat over low heat for about 2 minutes, or until the onion is translucent. Add the curry powder and cook for 1 minute. Add the apple and water and cook over low heat for 10 minutes, or until the apple is tender. Transfer to a high-speed blender, add the yogurt, and process until smooth. Season with ¼ teaspoon each salt and pepper.

To prepare the fennel: Combine the sliced fennel, fennel fronds, lemon juice, and ⅛ teaspoon each salt and pepper. Refrigerate for 30 minutes before using to allow the fennel to soften up.

ASSEMBLY

Place a slice of terrine on each plate and drizzle the Roasted Apple–Curry Sauce around the plate. Place some of the fennel mixture opposite the terrine. Garnish with the Herb Oil, if desired, orange pieces, and micro fennel sprouts. Top with pepper.

STEAMED PACIFIC MUSSELS WITH SAFFRON, FENNEL, AND TOMATO

This simple, quick-to-prepare dish is always a crowd-pleaser.

The juices released from the mussels during cooking add a briny, complex flavor to the saffron broth.

The hints of star anise and fennel are a welcome surprise on your palate.

SERVES 4

4 cups Vegetable Stock (see page 213)

¾ cup dry white wine

¼ teaspoon saffron threads

4 cloves garlic, smashed

2 bay leaves

1½ cups julienned fennel

2 tablespoons minced shallot

2 tablespoons chopped fennel fronds

1 tablespoon minced fresh chives

1½ cups diced tomato

Finely grated zest and juice of 2 lemons

1 teaspoon aniseeds, toasted and crushed

1 tablespoon chopped fresh tarragon

3 dozen Pacific mussels, scrubbed and debearded

Kosher salt and freshly ground pepper

METHOD

Place the stock, wine, saffron, garlic, bay leaves, julienned fennel, shallot, fennel fronds, chives, tomato, lemon zest and juice, aniseeds, and tarragon in a large saucepan and bring to a simmer. Add the mussels, cover, and cook for 2 to 3 minutes, or until the mussels have opened. Discard any mussels that failed to open. Season the broth with ½ teaspoon each salt and pepper.

ASSEMBLY

Divide the mussels and broth among 4 shallow bowls.

STEAMED STRIPED BASS WITH WILTED LETTUCES, TOMATO, CITRUS, AND HARICOTS VERTS

The citrus and tomato components in this dish are particularly refreshing, and they work

together successfully to heighten the flavor of the striped bass.

A poached or steamed chicken breast would be a splendid substitution for the fish.

SERVES 4

FOR THE FISH:

8 ½-ounce pieces striped bass fillet, skin removed
Kosher salt and freshly ground black pepper
4 cups loosely packed baby lettuces
½ lemon
2 teaspoons chopped fresh chives

FOR THE VEGETABLES:

2 tablespoons olive oil
1 tablespoon minced shallot
½ cup small-diced yellow tomato
20 haricots verts, blanched and cut in half
　on the bias
1 tablespoon freshly squeezed lemon juice
1 tablespoon freshly squeezed orange juice
⅓ cup orange segments, cut into thirds
2 tablespoons lime segments, cut into thirds
2 teaspoons chopped fresh chives

METHOD

To prepare the fish: Season the fish with ¼ teaspoon each salt and pepper. Place the fish on the bottom of a bamboo steamer basket, and place the basket over a pan of simmering water. Cover and steam for 5 to 7 minutes, or the fish is just opaque at the center. Remove the fish from the steamer basket and add the lettuces. Steam the lettuces for 30 seconds, or until they just begin to wilt. Remove the lettuces from the steamer basket and season to taste with salt and pepper. Squeeze the juice from the lemon half over the fish and lettuces. Sprinkle the chives over the fish.

To prepare the vegetables: Place the olive oil in a sauté pan over medium heat, add the shallot, and cook for 1 minute, or until the shallot is translucent. Add the tomato and haricots verts and cook for 2 minutes, or until tender. Add the lemon juice, orange juice, orange and lime segments, and chives, toss together until combined and warmed through, and remove from the heat.

ASSEMBLY

Place some of the wilted lettuces and the vegetables on each plate and set 2 pieces of fish over the lettuces. Spoon any juices that remain in the sauté pan around the plate.

VEGETABLE PAD THAI
WITH TOFU–KAFFIR LIME SAUCE

Once all the ingredients are measured and chopped, this dish comes together rather quickly.

And the result is definitely worth all the prep work!

You can also serve this dish spooned into lettuce leaves for a fun and flavorful appetizer.

SERVES 4

FOR THE TOFU–KAFFIR LIME SAUCE:

4 ounces firm silken tofu, chopped

1 tablespoon minced fresh ginger

1 clove garlic, smashed

2 kaffir lime leaves

1 red Thai chile

2 tablespoons freshly squeezed lemon juice

2 tablespoons maple syrup

1 tablespoon reduced-sodium soy sauce

¼ cup water, if needed to thin

FOR THE PAD THAI:

2 tablespoons tamarind juice (paste thinned with water)

1½ tablespoons maple syrup

1½ tablespoons reduced-sodium soy sauce

1½ teaspoons minced garlic

1¼ teaspoons minced, seeded serrano chile

1 tablespoon extra virgin olive oil

Kosher salt

6 ounces dried pad Thai rice noodles (about ¼ inch wide), cooked (scant 4 cups)

¾ cup julienned zucchini

¾ cup finely shredded red cabbage

¾ cup julienned carrot

¾ cup julienned red onion

¾ cup julienned Granny Smith apple, skin on

½ cup julienned red bell pepper

1 serrano chile, seeded and thinly sliced

2 tablespoons fresh cilantro leaves

FOR THE GARNISH:

2 teaspoons reduced-sodium soy sauce

2 teaspoons toasted sesame oil

¼ cup cashews, toasted and coarsely chopped

METHOD

To prepare the Tofu–Kaffir Lime Sauce: Combine the tofu, ginger, garlic, kaffir lime leaves, Thai chile, lemon juice, maple syrup, and soy sauce in a high-speed blender and blend until smooth, adding the water to thin if necessary. The sauce should be medium-bodied and smooth.

To prepare the Pad Thai: Combine the tamarind juice, maple syrup, soy sauce, garlic, minced serrano chile, olive oil, and ¼ teaspoon salt in a blender and process until smooth. Place the noodles, zucchini, cabbage, carrot, red onion, apple, bell pepper, sliced serrano chile, and cilantro in a bowl. Add the tamarind purée and half of the Tofu–Kaffir Lime Sauce and toss to coat.

ASSEMBLY

Spoon some of the remaining Tofu–Kaffir Lime Sauce down the center of each plate. Arrange the Pad Thai mixture on top of the sauce. Spoon ½ teaspoon each of the soy sauce and sesame oil around the Pad Thai. Sprinkle with the cashews.

GRILLED RAINBOW TROUT WITH
WILTED PEA SHOOTS AND WASABI-INFUSED PEA SAUCE

It is a joy when peas are tender and sweet. In this dish, they welcome the heat of the

wasabi and the aromatic bouquet of the basil. The pea sauce can easily be transformed into a soup, too,

by simply adding more peas and a bit of vegetable stock.

SERVES 4

FOR THE TROUT:

8 2-ounce pieces rainbow trout fillet, skin on
½ teaspoon olive oil
Kosher salt and freshly ground black pepper

FOR THE PEA SHOOTS:

4 cups loosely packed pea shoots
¼ cup water
Kosher salt and freshly ground black pepper
2 teaspoons olive oil
1 tablespoon freshly squeezed lemon juice
1 yellow tomato, peeled, seeded, and finely chopped
¼ cup shelled sugar snap peas, blanched
¼ Ruby Red grapefruit segments, chopped

FOR THE WASABI-INFUSED PEA SAUCE:

1 cup shelled sugar snap peas, blanched
6 fresh basil leaves
¼ cup freshly squeezed orange juice
1 teaspoon olive oil
1 teaspoon wasabi powder
Kosher salt and freshly ground black pepper

METHOD

To prepare the trout: Lightly brush the trout with the olive oil and season lightly with salt and pepper. Place the trout, skin side down, over a medium-hot fire and grill, turning once, for 2 to 3 minutes on each side, or just until opaque at the center.

To prepare the pea shoots: Place the pea shoots and water in a large sauté pan over medium-low heat and cook for 30 to 60 seconds, or until the pea shoots wilt. Season with ¼ teaspoon each salt and pepper, then transfer the pea shoots to a plate. Add the olive oil, lemon juice, tomato, peas, and grapefruit to the sauté pan and cook over low heat just until hot. Return the pea shoots to the pan, heat through briefly, and season lightly with salt and pepper.

To prepare the Wasabi-Infused Pea Sauce: Combine the peas, basil, orange juice, olive oil, and wasabi powder in a blender and process until smooth. Season with ¼ teaspoon each salt and pepper and warm in a small saucepan just before serving.

ASSEMBLY

Spoon some of the Wasabi-Infused Pea Sauce onto the center of each plate. Remove a few pea shoots from the pea shoots–tomato mixture and reserve them for garnish. Spoon some of the pea shoots–tomato mixture over the sauce on each plate, and shingle 2 pieces of the fish on top. Arrange the reserved pea shoots over the fish and top with pepper.

BIGEYE TUNA WITH ARTICHOKES, NIÇOISE OLIVES, AND CORIANDER-CAPER VINAIGRETTE

This salad draws on the classic salade niçoise for its inspiration.

But here I have added aromatic coriander,

toothsome artichokes, and briny capers to round out the flavors.

SERVES 4

FOR THE TUNA:
12 ounces bigeye tuna loin
1 teaspoon olive oil
Kosher salt and freshly ground black pepper

FOR THE CORIANDER-CAPER
VINAIGRETTE:
1½ tablespoons olive oil
1 tablespoon balsamic vinegar
1 tablespoon low-sodium chicken broth
1½ tablespoons capers, rinsed and chopped
1 tablespoon chopped fresh chives
¾ teaspoon coriander seeds, toasted
*   and coarsely ground*
Kosher salt and freshly ground black pepper

FOR THE VEGETABLES:
4 Braised Artichokes, each cut into 6 wedges
*   through the stem (see page 207)*
½ cup niçoise olives, pitted and quartered
4 cups loosely packed baby spinach leaves
10 ounces haricots verts, blanched
1 cup yellow Teardrop tomatoes, cut in
*   half lengthwise*
¼ cup thinly sliced red onion

Freshly ground black pepper

METHOD

To prepare the tuna: Rub the tuna with the olive oil and season with ⅛ teaspoon each salt and pepper. Place over a medium-hot fire and grill for 3 minutes on each side, or until medium or medium-rare. Thinly slice the tuna and season with ⅛ teaspoon each salt and pepper.

To prepare the Coriander-Caper Vinaigrette: Combine the olive oil, vinegar, broth, capers, chives, and coriander in a small bowl and whisk together. Season with ¼ teaspoon each salt and pepper.

To prepare the vegetables: Combine the Braised Artichokes, olives, spinach, haricots verts, tomatoes, and red onion in a bowl and toss to mix. Just before serving, toss the vegetables with half of the Coriander-Caper Vinaigrette.

ASSEMBLY

Arrange the vegetables in the center of each plate and lay the tuna slices over the vegetables. Spoon the remaining vinaigrette over the tuna and around the plate. Top with pepper.

SEA SCALLOPS WITH BUTTERNUT SQUASH PURÉE AND CURRY-FENNEL EMULSION

The scallops nest in the butternut squash, which provides the perfect foundation for the light

and airy curry-infused fennel emulsion. If a lighter preparation is desired, the butternut squash can be blended with

some Vegetable Stock to create a soup that can poured around the scallops and emulsion tableside.

SERVES 4

FOR THE FENNEL JUICE:
3 cups fresh fennel juice (4 to 5 large fennel bulbs)

FOR THE CURRY BUTTER:
1 teaspoon grapeseed oil
¼ cup diced Spanish onion
¼ cup peeled, diced Granny Smith apple
1 tablespoon yellow curry powder
½ cup water
2 tablespoons unsalted butter, softened

FOR THE CURRY-FENNEL EMULSION:
Fennel Juice (above)
1 small Granny Smith apple, peeled and chopped
3 tablespoons Curry Butter (above)
2 tablespoons freshly squeezed lemon juice
Kosher salt and freshly ground black pepper

FOR THE BUTTERNUT SQUASH:
1 butternut squash
Kosher salt and freshly ground black pepper

FOR THE SCALLOPS:
12 large sea scallops, muscle trimmed
1 clove garlic, minced
2 teaspoons fennel fronds, minced
1 teaspoon finely grated lemon zest
Kosher salt and freshly ground black pepper
2 teaspoons grapeseed oil

2 teaspoons minced fennel fronds

METHOD

To prepare the fennel juice: Place the fennel juice in a small saucepan and simmer over medium heat for 15 to 20 minutes, or until it looks separated. Strain through a fine-mesh sieve lined with cheesecloth into a bowl. Refrigerate until needed.

To prepare the Curry Butter: Heat the grapeseed oil in a small saucepan over medium heat, add the onion, and sauté for 3 to 4 minutes, or until translucent. Add the apple, curry powder, and water and continue to cook, stirring occasionally, for 10 minutes, or until the apple is soft and tender. Let cool, purée in a food processor, and pass through a fine-mesh sieve. Fold into the softened butter and refrigerate until needed.

To prepare the Curry-Fennel Emulsion: Place the Fennel Juice in a small saucepan and simmer for 10 to 15 minutes, or until reduced to 1 cup. Add the apple, simmer for 5 minutes, and strain through a fine-mesh sieve. Just before serving, whisk in the Curry Butter and lemon juice. Season to taste with salt and pepper and keep warm. Froth with a handheld blender just before serving.

To prepare the butternut squash: Preheat the oven to 350 degrees. Halve the butternut squash and discard the seeds. Rub the cut side of both halves with some salt and pepper. Place the halves, cut side down, in a baking pan and roast for 30 minutes, or until tender. Scoop out the flesh into a saucepan, discarding the peel, and mash coarsely with a fork. Warm over medium heat just before using.

To prepare the scallops: Place the scallops, garlic, fennel fronds, and lemon zest in a resealable plastic bag. Seal the bag closed and marinate the scallops in the refrigerator for 20 minutes. Remove the scallops from the marinade and discard the marinade. Lightly season both sides of the scallops with salt and pepper. Heat the grapeseed oil in a sauté pan over medium-high heat. Add the scallops and sauté quickly, turning once, for 1 to 2 minutes on each side, or just until cooked.

ASSEMBLY

Place a mound of the butternut squash in the center of each bowl and arrange 3 scallops on top. Ladle some of the Curry-Fennel Emulsion into each bowl, and sprinkle with the minced fennel fronds.

GRILLED ONO WITH QUINOA, SUNCHOKES, AND CHARRED EGGPLANT

Charring the eggplant on the grill results in its flesh taking on a smoky essence. The eggplant is the star in this dish, but it shares the spotlight with the tender sunchokes and nutty-tasting quinoa. If white, flaky ono, a prized Hawaiian fish also known as wahoo, is not available in your market, you may substitute any firm, lean white fish.

SERVES 4

FOR THE ONO:
8 2-ounce pieces ono fillet, skin removed
Olive oil (optional)
Kosher salt and freshly ground black pepper

FOR THE SUNCHOKES:
2 sunchokes, peeled and cut into small dice
1 cup Vegetable Stock (see page 213)
2 sprigs thyme
2 tablespoons freshly squeezed lemon juice
Kosher salt and freshly ground black pepper

FOR THE EGGPLANT:
1 eggplant
1 tablespoon olive oil
2 tablespoons roasted garlic
Kosher salt and freshly ground black pepper

FOR THE QUINOA:
2 cups cooked quinoa, warm
1/3 cup brunoise-cut cucumber, skin on
1 tablespoon chopped fresh chives
1 tablespoon chopped fresh flat-leaf parsley
1 tablespoon olive oil
2 tablespoons freshly squeezed lemon juice
Kosher salt and freshly ground black pepper

1 tablespoon long-cut fresh chives

METHOD

To prepare the ono: Lightly brush the ono with olive oil, if desired, and season lightly with salt and pepper. Grill the ono over a medium-hot fire, turning once, for 2 to 3 minutes on each side, or just until opaque at the center.

To prepare the sunchokes: Place the sunchokes, Vegetable Stock, thyme, and 1 tablespoon of the lemon juice in a saucepan and simmer over medium-low heat for about 10 minutes, or until the sunchokes are just tender. Drain the sunchokes just before using, toss with the remaining 1 tablespoon lemon juice, and season to taste with salt and pepper.

To prepare the eggplant: Grill the eggplant over a medium-hot fire, turning once, for about 10 minutes on each side, or until fully charred on all sides. Let cool and cut open. Scrape out the flesh, discarding the skin, and transfer to a bowl. Add the olive oil and roasted garlic and mix well. Season with ¼ teaspoon each salt and pepper.

To prepare the quinoa: Place the quinoa, cucumber, chives, parsley, olive oil, and lemon juice in a bowl and mix well. Season to taste with salt and pepper.

ASSEMBLY

Arrange some of the quinoa and sunchokes in the center of each plate. Spoon the eggplant around the quinoa, and top the quinoa with 2 pieces of fish. Sprinkle the long-cut chives over the fish.

GRILLED PHEASANT BREAST WITH STRAWBERRIES, APRICOTS AND PISTACHIOS

If you are lucky enough to find wild strawberries, or fraises des bois, *this dish will satisfy even the toughest critics. The strawberries and apricots blend together smoothly, yet still keep their identities intact. The curry element in the sauce is subtle enough to let the fruits be the true stars. Chicken or salmon would be a satisfying substitute for the pheasant.*

SERVES 4

FOR THE LEEKS:
4 pencil leeks, trimmed
¼ cup water
Kosher salt and freshly ground black pepper
4 wild strawberries, stems removed and
*   cut into small dice*

FOR THE APRICOTS:
4 apricots, peeled, pitted, and sliced
¼ cup Chicken Stock (see page 207)
12 wild strawberries, stems on, cut in half
*   lengthwise*

FOR THE PHEASANT:
3 boneless, skinless pheasant breast halves
Kosher salt and freshly ground black pepper
1 teaspoon olive oil

FOR THE GARNISH:
¼ cup Apricot Curry Sauce (see page 206)
4 teaspoons pistachio nuts, toasted and chopped
2 teaspoons fresh spearmint chiffonade
Freshly ground black pepper

METHOD

To prepare the pencil leeks: Place the leeks and water in a small saucepan and cook over medium heat for 3 minutes, or until the leeks are tender. Remove the leeks from the pan, leaving the liquid in the pan. Cut the leeks on the diagonal into 1-inch pieces, and season with ¼ teaspoon each salt and pepper. Add the diced strawberries to the liquid remaining in the pan and cook over low heat for 2 minutes, or until warm and just softened. Remove two-thirds of the strawberries from the pan with a slotted spoon and set aside. Pass the remaining strawberries and liquid through a fine-mesh sieve, and reserve the resulting strawberry juice for garnish.

To prepare the apricots: Warm the apricots in the Chicken Stock in a small saucepan for 5 minutes, or until the apricots are tender. Add the halved strawberries and toss lightly to warm.

To prepare the pheasant: Season the pheasant breasts with ⅛ teaspoon each salt and pepper and rub with the olive oil. Grill the pheasant over a medium-hot fire, turning once, for 4 minutes on each side, or just until cooked. Remove from the grill and let rest for 3 minutes, then thinly slice to yield 20 to 28 slices total. Season the pheasant slices with ⅛ teaspoon each salt and pepper.

ASSEMBLY

Arrange some of the pencil leeks, reserved diced strawberries, and apricots in the center of each plate. Lay 5 to 7 pheasant slices over the leeks. Spoon some of the Apricot Curry Sauce, strawberry juice, and any juice from the apricots around the plate. Sprinkle with the pistachios and spearmint and top with pepper.

GRILLED BEEF TENDERLOIN WITH TOMATO-AND-LEEK-STREWN QUINOA AND ROASTED GARLIC SAUCE

The leek-laced quinoa is the ultimate side dish to almost any grilled meat or fish. I have also enjoyed

leftovers of this dish chilled for lunch the next day. I chop the beef and fold it

into the quinoa along with the garlic sauce and leeks—a delightful and easy-to-make meal!

SERVES 6

FOR THE ROASTED GARLIC SAUCE:
2 bulbs garlic, tops cut off
2 cups skim milk
½ cup olive oil
½ cup Chicken Stock (see page 207)
1 teaspoon sherry vinegar
Kosher salt and freshly ground black pepper

FOR THE BEEF:
1½ pounds beef tenderloin, trimmed
1 tablespoon olive oil
Kosher salt and freshly ground black pepper

FOR THE QUINOA:
3 tablespoons olive oil
2 cups chopped leek
¼ cup Chicken Stock (see page 207)
1 yellow tomato, seeded and diced
2½ cups cooked quinoa
1 tablespoon freshly squeezed lemon juice
1½ tablespoons sherry vinegar
2 tablespoons chopped scallion
2 tablespoons chopped fresh basil
Kosher salt and freshly ground black pepper

4 teaspoons long-cut fresh chives
Freshly ground black pepper

METHOD

To prepare the Roasted Garlic Sauce: Preheat the oven to 350 degrees. Combine the garlic bulbs and milk in a small saucepan and simmer for 10 minutes. Drain the garlic, discarding the milk. Place the garlic bulbs upright in a small baking pan or dish and add the olive oil. Cover with a tight-fitting lid or aluminum foil and bake for 1½ hours, or until the garlic bulbs are soft. Let the garlic cool in the oil, then discard the oil or save for another use. Squeeze the soft garlic pulp out of the skins. Combine the garlic, stock, and vinegar in a blender and process until smooth. Season with ⅛ teaspoon each salt and pepper. Reheat gently just before using.

To prepare the beef: Rub the beef with the olive oil and season with ¼ teaspoon each salt and pepper. Grill the beef over a medium-hot fire for 10 minutes on each side, or until medium-rare. Remove the beef from the grill and let rest for 3 minutes. Slice the beef into ⅓-inch-thick slices, and season the slices with ¼ teaspoon each salt and pepper.

To prepare the quinoa: Heat 1 tablespoon of the olive oil in a large sauté pan over medium heat. Add the leek and cook for 3 minutes, or until light golden brown. Add the stock and continue to cook for 3 to 5 minutes, or until the leek is tender. Remove the leek from the pan and reserve for garnish. Add the tomato to the same pan, return to medium heat, and cook for 2 minutes. Add the remaining 2 tablespoons olive oil, the quinoa, lemon juice, vinegar, scallion, and basil and stir until all the ingredients are evenly distributed and warm. Season with ⅛ teaspoon each salt and pepper.

ASSEMBLY

Spoon some of the quinoa mixture in the center of each plate and arrange some of the beef slices over the quinoa. Spoon the Roasted Garlic Sauce around the plate. Spoon some of the reserved leeks on the top side of the plate alongside the beef. Sprinkle the chives over the beef and top with pepper.

SHABU-SHABU WITH DRY-AGED BEEF STRIP LOIN AND MUSHROOM BROTH

Traditional preparations of shabu-shabu are cooked tableside, with the noodles added once the beef and vegetables have been cooked in the broth. In this recipe, I serve the dish already finished, so that my guests can enjoy the shabu-shabu without doing any of the work! Be spontaneous with the ingredients, customizing the recipe to satisfy your cravings.

SERVES 4

3 cups Mushroom Broth (see page 209)

2 tablespoons chopped fresh ginger

1 jalapeño chile, seeded and minced

2 tablespoons reduced-sodium soy sauce

1 tablespoon toasted sesame oil

2 tablespoons ponzu sauce

3 ounces dried soba noodles, cooked (2 cups)

1 cup julienned shiitake mushroom

2 cups loosely packed 2-inch-pieces bok choy
    or cabbage

8 ounces firm silken tofu, cut into small dice

¾ cup peeled, grated daikon

1 pound well-trimmed beef strip loin, thinly sliced

4 scallions, green tops only, finely chopped

1 tablespoon fresh cilantro leaves

½ lime

METHOD

To prepare the shabu-shabu broth: Place the Mushroom Broth in a saucepan and bring to a simmer. Add the ginger, chile, soy sauce, sesame oil, and ponzu sauce and simmer for 3 minutes.

ASSEMBLY

Arrange some of the soba noodles in the center of each bowl. Place a small mound of the mushroom, bok choy, tofu, and daikon at separate points around the bowl. Place the beef around the bowl and ladle in the hot broth over the beef. Sprinkle the scallions and cilantro around the bowl and squeeze the lime half over the broth.

GRILLED PINEAPPLE WITH CRYSTALLIZED GINGER, COCONUT EMULSION, AND COCONUT SORBET

In summertime, I like to grill fresh fruits and melons, especially over hickory and cedar chips. Once the fruit is grilled, you can use it immediately or you can chill it for the ultimate summer refreshment. I use coconut along with the pineapple in this dessert, but the portion is not excessive. A little indulgence, like the coconut here, is always acceptable.

SERVES 4

COCONUT SORBET

Water and meat from 1 young Thai coconut
3 tablespoons Sucanat (unrefined cane sugar)
or sugar

FOR THE PINEAPPLE:

8 ½-inch-thick pineapple slices, cored
Seeds from ½ vanilla bean

FOR THE COCONUT EMULSION:

½ cup coconut milk

FOR THE GARNISH:

2 tablespoons julienned crystallized ginger
2 tablespoons ground fresh coconut, toasted

METHOD

To prepare the Coconut Sorbet: Combine the coconut water, meat, and Sucanat in a high-speed blender and process until smooth. Pass the purée through a fine-mesh sieve and freeze in an ice-cream maker. Store in a tightly sealed container in the freezer for up to 2 weeks.

To prepare the pineapple: Rub the pineapple with the vanilla bean seeds. Place over a medium-hot fire and grill, turning once, for 4 to 5 minutes on each side, or until the pineapple begins to caramelize. Remove the pineapple from the grill and cut into 2-inch lengths, reserving any juices that accumulate for garnish.

To prepare the Coconut Emulsion: Place the coconut milk in a small saucepan and warm gently over medium-low heat just until warm. Remove from the heat and froth the warm coconut milk with a handheld blender just before using.

ASSEMBLY

Arrange some of the pineapple pieces and crystallized ginger in each shallow bowl. Drizzle any reserved juices over the pineapple. Place a small amount of the toasted coconut on the pineapple, and set a large quenelle of the Coconut Sorbet on the toasted coconut. Spoon the Coconut Emulsion around the pineapple, and sprinkle the plate with more toasted coconut.

PASSION FRUIT PUDDING CAKE

Pudding cake is too often an underappreciated dessert. I look forward to every spoonful of the creamy custard and silky cake. It can be made a few days in advance without losing any of its freshness, and it fully embraces nearly any flavoring you might want to incorporate, including the passion fruit used here, but also lemon, green tea, or even chocolate.

SERVES 16

FOR THE PUDDING CAKE:
4 tablespoons unsalted butter, softened
1 cup plus 2 tablespoons sugar
Pinch of kosher salt
6 egg yolks
6 tablespoons flour
2 cups skim milk
½ cup fresh passion fruit juice
8 egg whites

FOR THE GARNISH:
2 passion fruits
¾ cup nonfat plain yogurt
1 tablespoon honey
4 teaspoons honeycomb
1 cup wild strawberries, stems on, large berries
  cut in half lengthwise

METHOD

To make the pudding cake: Preheat the oven to 325 degrees. Line a quarter sheet pan (8½ by 12 inches) with plastic wrap. Combine the butter, sugar, and salt in a large bowl and cream with an electric mixer until smooth and fluffy. Add the egg yolks one at a time, mixing well after each addition. Add the flour and mix well. Add the milk and passion fruit juice and mix until combined. In a separate mixer bowl, beat the egg whites until stiff peaks form. Gently fold the egg whites into the batter just until combined. Immediately pour the batter into the prepared sheet pan. Place the sheet pan in a large roasting pan and add hot water to the roasting pan to reach halfway up the sides of the sheet pan. Bake for about 45 minutes, or until golden brown and firm to the touch. Carefully remove the sheet pan from the water bath and let the cake cool to room temperature, then refrigerate until well chilled. To unmold, invert onto a cutting board, lift off the pan, and peel off the plastic wrap. Trim all 4 edges to even them, and then cut the cake into 16 pieces, each 4 by 1½ inches.

To prepare the garnish: Cut the passion fruits in half and scoop the seeds and juice into a bowl. Add the yogurt and honey and stir until combined.

ASSEMBLY

Place a piece of the chilled pudding cake on each plate. Drizzle 1 tablespoon of the passion fruit–yogurt sauce over the cake and around the plate. Place ¼ teaspoon of the honeycomb in front of the cake, and sprinkle the strawberries around the plate.

CHILLED CHOCOLATE-ORANGE SOUFFLÉ
WITH CHOCOLATE SORBET

This soufflé reminds me of floating island, the classic dessert of meringue clouds in a custard sauce.

But my version has about half the amount of sugar and calls for intensely flavored cocoa powder.

You can make the soufflé in the morning and serve it that evening to your guests.

SERVES 6

FOR THE SOUFFLÉS:
Nonstick cooking spray
4 egg whites
½ teaspoon cream of tartar
¼ cup Sucanat (unrefined cane sugar) or sugar
1 tablespoon cocoa powder
1 orange

FOR THE CHOCOLATE SAUCE:
2 tablespoons boiling water
1 ounce 70% bittersweet chocolate, chopped

FOR THE GARNISH:
Segments from 1 orange, juices reserved
½ cup plus 1 tablespoon Chocolate Sorbet
    (see page 207)
1 tablespoon fresh tiny mint leaves

METHOD

To prepare the soufflés: Preheat the oven to 350 degrees. Spray 6 round soufflé molds, each 2¾ inches in diameter and 1¾ inches deep, with nonstick cooking spray. Put the egg whites in a mixer bowl, add the cream of tartar, and whisk until frothy. Using the mixer, whip the egg whites to soft peaks while adding the Sucanat 1 tablespoon at a time. Sift the cocoa powder over the whites, then finely grate the zest of the orange over the whites. Gently fold in the cocoa and zest. Fill the prepared molds to the rim with the soufflé batter. Place the molds in a large baking pan, and add boiling water to reach halfway up the sides of the molds. Bake for 20 minutes, or until the soufflés rise and do not leave a fingerprint when the tops are gently touched. Let cool and then chill before serving. Do not umold until ready to use.

To prepare the Chocolate Sauce: Pour the boiling water over the chocolate in a small bowl and whisk until smooth.

ASSEMBLY

Invert 1 soufflé onto the center of each plate, allowing any juices in the mold to drip onto the plate. (If a soufflé resists unmolding, carefully loosen the sides with a paring knife and then invert.) Drizzle some Chocolate Sauce over the soufflé and around the plate. Place a few orange segments and the reserved juices around the soufflé, and set a quenelle of the sorbet on top of the orange segments. Sprinkle the mint over the plate.

Morning

PAGE	RECIPE	CALORIES	PROTEIN (g)	
86	Coconut, Lemongrass, and Pineapple Smoothie	85	4	
86	Peach Lemonade	135	0	
88	Asian Pear, Prickly Pear, and Kaffir Lime Infusion	90	1	
88	Heirloom Tomato and Basil Water	20	1	
88	Cucumber and Mint Smoothie	55	3	
89	Mango and Kaffir Lime Leaf Smoothie	85	3	
89	Chocolate, Banana, and Yogurt Smoothie	140	8	
89	Cucumber, Mint, Apple, and Key Lime Juice	65	2	
92	Egg White Omelet with Cold-Smoked Sturgeon and Stewed Radishes	140	21	
95	Warm Miso Soup with Silken Tofu, Soft Poached Egg, and Glass Noodles	250	13	
96	Whole-Wheat Pancakes with Maui Onion Marmalade and Stewed Strawberries	235	8	
99	Tropical Fruits with Lavender-Mint Yogurt and Toasted Almonds	280	13	
100	Soft Poached Egg with Cured Salmon, Baby Spinach, and an Olive Oil and Lemon Zest Vinaigrette	155	11	

All of the recipes in this book have been analyzed for the primary nutrients they contain, and these nutritional values, calculated per serving, are shown here. The computations do not reflect optional ingredients, such as some herb-flavored oils; alternative ingredients, such as a second type of cheese; or ingredients added to taste, such as salt and pepper. In the case of the latter, many recipes include specific amounts of salt and pepper and also call for seasoning to taste. In these instances, only the specified amounts have been used for the nutritional calculations. If you are on a sodium-restricted diet or have other dietary concerns, consult your doctor or a registered dietitian before including any of these recipes in your daily regimen.

COMPLEX CARBOHYDRATES (mg)	FAT (g)	CHOLESTEROL (g)	SATURATED FAT (g)	MONO- UNSATURATED FAT (g)	POLY- UNSATURATED FAT (g)	SODIUM (mg)	FIBER (g)
17	0	0	0	0	0	85	1.3
36	0	0	0	0	0	5	0.1
22	0	0	0	0	0	5	2.8
5	0	0	0	0	0	140	0
11	0	0	0	0	0	35	0.5
19	0	0	0	0	0	35	1.7
25	0	0	0	0	0	160	3.4
15	0	0	0	0	0	25	2
3	5	30	1.5	2	0.5	400	1.1
28	9	315	2.5	3	1.5	885	1.6
39	6	45	1	4	1	265	4.6
48	5	5	1	3	1	140	4.5
6	9	215	1.5	5	0.5	695	2.3

Midday

COMPLEX CARBOHYDRATES (mg)	FAT (g)	CHOLESTEROL (g)	SATURATED FAT (g)	MONO-UNSATURATED FAT (g)	POLY-UNSATURATED FAT (g)	SODIUM (mg)	FIBER (g)
6	4	50	0.5	1.5	1	1,220	1
23	3	0	0.5	1.5	1	115	2.6
14	8	0	1	5	1	215	3.6
35	6	0	1	0.5	0.5	100	4.5
10	8	55	1.5	4	2	475	2.6
11	7	25	0.5	2	4.5	300	3.2
30	11	10	3	5.5	1	333	8.5
44	3	0	0.5	1	1	950	3.2
12	17	70	3	8	5	510	2.4
10	7	265	1	3	2	565	0.8
37	5	65	1	3	2	880	6.5
32	18	85	3	10.5	3	295	3.2
26	0	0	0	0	0	25	5
13	1	0	0	0	0.5	50	3
23	1	0	0	0	0.5	60	1.5

Evening

COMPLEX CARBOHYDRATES (mg)	FAT (g)	CHOLESTEROL (g)	SATURATED FAT (g)	MONO- UNSATURATED FAT (g)	POLY- UNSATURATED FAT (g)	SODIUM (mg)	FIBER (g)
22	12	10	4	6	1.5	175	7.9
11	3	215	0.5	1.5	0.5	215	1.7
23	4	50	1	1	1	650	4.6
8	9	70	1.5	5.5	1.5	140	2.3
43	8	0	1.5	3.5	1	1,015	3.6
9	13	75	3.5	5.5	3.5	215	2
19	12	30	2	7	2	500	9.8
34	8	40	1.5	2.5	3	625	4
34	10	45	2	4.5	2	185	5.8
14	7	80	2	3	1.5	195	2
26	20	70	4.5	11	2	200	2.4
23	19	55	6	7	5	610	2.3
42	9	5	7.5	0.5	0	20	2.3
22	5	85	2.4	1.5	0.5	60	0.5
23	4	0	2	1	0	50	2.4

APRICOT CURRY SAUCE

YIELD: 2 ½ CUPS;
20 2-TABLESPOON SERVINGS

½ cup dried apricots
1½ teaspoons hot curry powder
⅓ cup rice vinegar
1½ cups water

METHOD

Combine the apricots, curry powder, vinegar, and water in a blender and process until smooth. Refrigerate overnight, then strain through a fine-mesh sieve the next day. Return to the refrigerator until ready to use. It will keep for up to 1 week.

BASIL OIL

YIELD: ½ CUP;
8 1-TABLESPOON SERVINGS

¾ cup firmly packed basil leaves
½ cup grapeseed oil
¼ cup olive oil

METHOD

Place the basil leaves with 1 tablespoon of the grapeseed oil in a small sauté pan and sauté over medium heat for 2 minutes, or until wilted. Shock immediately in ice water and drain. Coarsely chop the basil and squeeze out the excess water. Transfer to a high-speed blender, add the remaining 7 tablespoons grapeseed oil and the olive oil, and process for 3 to 4 minutes, or until bright green. Pour into a container, cover, and refrigerate for 1 day.

Strain the oil through a fine-mesh sieve and discard the solids. Refrigerate for 1 day, decant, and refrigerate until ready to use or for up to 2 weeks.

BRAISED ARTICHOKES

YIELD: 4 ARTICHOKES BOTTOMS
WITH STEMS ATTACHED;
4 SERVINGS

4 artichokes
1 cup chopped carrot
1 cup chopped celery
1 cup chopped Spanish onion
1 lemon, cut in half
2 bay leaves

METHOD

Trim off all of the leaves from each artichoke flush with the base, and then trim and peel the stem. Combine the artichoke bottoms, carrot, celery, onion, lemon, and bay leaves in a saucepan, add water to cover, and bring to a simmer. Cover with a piece of parchment paper or a kitchen towel to weigh down the artichokes and cook over low heat for 30 to 40 minutes, or until the artichokes are just tender. A knife should slide easily into the artichoke, though you should feel slight resistance. Remove the artichokes from the liquid, scrape out the chokes, and store in the refrigerator for up to 3 days.

CHICKEN STOCK

YIELD: 2 QUARTS;
8 1-CUP SERVINGS

6 pounds meaty chicken bones
3 cups chopped Spanish onion
2 cups chopped carrot
2 cups chopped celery
1 cup chopped leek
1 tablespoon white peppercorns
1 bay leaf

METHOD

Place the chicken bones, onion, carrot, celery, leek, peppercorns, and bay leaf in a stockpot and add cold water to cover by three-quarters. Bring to a boil, reduce the heat to low, and simmer slowly, uncovered, for 4 hours, skimming every 30 minutes to remove impurities that rise to the surface. Strain through a fine-mesh sieve and then continue to cook, uncovered, over medium heat for 30 to 45 minutes, or until reduced to 2 quarts. Store in the refrigerator for up to 4 days or freeze for up to 2 months.

CHOCOLATE SORBET

YIELD: 1 QUART;
42 1½-TABLESPOON SERVINGS

7 ounces 70% bittersweet chocolate,
    chopped
9½ tablespoons Sucanat (unrefined
    cane sugar) or sugar
2 tablespoons plus 2 teaspoons
    cocoa powder
1 cup water
⅔ cup freshly brewed coffee
½ cup freshly squeezed orange juice
1 tablespoon light corn syrup

METHOD

Combine the chocolate, Sucanat, and cocoa powder in a heatproof bowl. Combine the water, coffee, orange juice, and corn syrup in a small saucepan, bring to a boil, and pour over the chocolate mixture. Whisk until smooth and then cool over an ice bath. Freeze in an ice-cream maker. Store in a tightly sealed container in the freezer for up to 2 weeks.

COURT BOUILLON

YIELD: 3 CUPS;
4 ¾-CUP SERVINGS

2¼ cups water
¾ cup dry white wine
Juice of 1 lemon
1 Spanish onion, chopped
1 celery stalk, chopped
2 cloves garlic
1 teaspoon black peppercorns
5 sprigs thyme
1 bay leaf

METHOD

Combine the water, wine, lemon juice, onion, celery, garlic, peppercorns, thyme, and bay leaf in a saucepan and bring to a boil over high heat. Reduce the heat to a simmer and cook for 8 minutes. Strain through a fine-mesh sieve. Store in the refrigerator for up to 3 days or freeze for up to 1 month.

HERB OIL

YIELD: ½ CUP;
8 1-TABLESPOON SERVINGS

¼ cup firmly packed chopped fresh chives
¼ cup firmly packed fresh flat-leaf
    parsley leaves
¼ cup firmly packed watercress leaves
½ cup grapeseed oil
¼ cup olive oil

METHOD

Place the chives, parsley, and watercress with 1 tablespoon of the grapeseed oil in a small sauté pan and sauté over medium heat for 2 minutes, or until wilted. Shock immediately in ice water and drain. Coarsely chop the mixture and squeeze out the excess water. Transfer to a high-speed blender, add the remaining 7 tablespoons grapeseed oil and the olive oil, and process for 3 to 4 minutes, or until bright green. Pour into a container, cover, and refrigerate for 1 day.

Strain the oil through a fine-mesh sieve and discard the solids. Refrigerate for 1 day, decant, and refrigerate until ready to use or for up to 2 weeks.

MAUI ONION MARMALADE

YIELD: 1 CUP;
8 2-TABLESPOON SERVINGS

1 tablespoon extra virgin olive oil
3 Maui onions, finely diced
1 tablespoon brown sugar
Kosher salt and freshly ground black pepper
¾ cup cider vinegar
1 cup unsweetened apple juice
2 tablespoons chopped fresh chives

METHOD

Heat the olive oil in a large, heavy-bottomed saucepan over medium heat and add the onions. Cook, stirring, for about 10 minutes, or until the onions begin to soften. Add the brown sugar, stir to coat the onions, and season with ¼ teaspoon salt and ⅛ teaspoon pepper. Continue cooking over medium heat, stirring frequently, for 10 to 15 minutes longer, or until the onions begin to turn golden brown. Add the vinegar and cook, stirring, for 10 to 15 minutes, or until the vinegar has evaporated. Add the apple juice and continue to cook, stirring frequently to prevent sticking and burning, for 15 to 20 minutes, or until it has evaporated. Season the marmalade to taste with salt and pepper. Remove from the heat, fold in the chives, and serve warm. Store in the refrigerator for up to 3 days.

MUSHROOM BROTH

YIELD: 1½ QUARTS;
6 ½-CUP SERVINGS

1 pound white button or cremini mushrooms
2 portobello mushrooms
8 shiitake mushrooms
1 cup chopped Spanish onion
1 bulb garlic, cloves separated and peeled
3 sprigs thyme
3½ quarts water

METHOD

Combine the mushrooms, onion, garlic, thyme, and water in a saucepan, bring to boil, reduce the heat to medium-low, and simmer for 1½ hours. Strain through a fine-mesh sieve. Store in the refrigerator for up to 4 days or freeze for up to 2 months.

PRESERVED GINGER

YIELD: 4 TEASPOONS;
4 1-TEASPOON SERVINGS

4 teaspoons julienned fresh ginger
½ cup sugar
2 cups water

METHOD

Place the ginger, 2 tablespoons of the sugar, and ½ cup of the water in a small saucepan. Bring to a simmer and simmer for 10 minutes. Drain the ginger, discarding the liquid, and return the ginger to the saucepan. Add 2 tablespoons of the sugar and ½ cup of the water and again simmer for 10 minutes. Repeat two more times, then remove from the heat, let cool, and refrigerate the ginger in the liquid for up to 2 weeks. Drain off the liquid before using the ginger.

ROASTED MUSHROOMS

YIELD: ABOUT 2 CUPS;
4 ½-CUP SERVINGS

3 cups assorted mushrooms, such as
    shiitake, cremini, black trumpet,
    hedgehog, and portobello,
    or a single type, stems removed
½ cup chopped Spanish onion
1 clove garlic
1 sprig thyme or rosemary
¾ cup Mushroom Broth (see page 209)
    or water
Kosher salt and freshly
    ground black pepper

METHOD

Preheat the oven to 325 degrees. Place the mushrooms in a baking pan and toss with the onion, garlic, and thyme. Add the Mushroom Broth and season with ¼ teaspoon each salt and pepper. Cover and bake for 30 to 40 minutes, or until the mushrooms are tender. Remove from the oven and let cool in the cooking juices. Store in the refrigerator for up to 3 days.

SHELLFISH STOCK

YIELD: 2 QUARTS;
8 1-CUP SERVINGS

5 pounds lobster shells
2 tablespoons canola oil
½ cup chopped carrot
½ cup chopped celery
1 cup chopped leek
2 tablespoons tomato paste
1 cup full-bodied red wine

METHOD

Preheat the oven to 400 degrees. Place the lobster shells in a roasting pan and roast for 40 minutes, or until bright red and lightly golden brown.

Heat the canola oil in a stockpot over medium-high heat. Add the carrot, celery, and leek and sauté for 10 minutes, or until golden brown and caramelized. Add the tomato paste and cook for 2 to 3 minutes. Deglaze the pan with the wine and cook for 3 minutes, or until most of the red wine has been absorbed. Add the lobster shells and then add cold water to cover by three-quarters. Bring to a boil, reduce the heat to low, and simmer slowly, uncovered, for 3 hours, skimming every 30 minutes to remove impurities that rise to the surface. Strain through a fine-mesh sieve and then continue to cook, uncovered, over medium-low heat for 20 to 25 minutes, or until reduced to 2 quarts. Store in the refrigerator for up to 1 week or freeze for up to 1 month.

SIMPLE SYRUP

YIELD: 1 ½ CUPS;
24 1-TABLESPOON SERVINGS

1½ cups sugar
1½ cups water

METHOD

Combine the sugar and water in a small saucepan and bring to a boil, stirring often until the sugar has dissolved. Remove from the heat, let cool, and refrigerate for up to 1 month.

VEGETABLE STOCK

YIELD: 2 QUARTS;
8 1-CUP SERVINGS

1 cup chopped Spanish onion
1 cup chopped carrot
1 cup chopped celery
1 cup chopped fennel
1 red bell pepper, seeded and chopped
3 cloves garlic
½ cup chopped parsnip
1 bay leaf
1 teaspoon black peppercorns
4 quarts water

METHOD

Place the onion, carrot, celery, fennel, bell pepper, garlic, parsnip, bay leaf, peppercorns, and water in a stockpot and bring to a boil. Reduce the heat to medium-low and simmer slowly, uncovered, for 1 hour. Strain through a fine-mesh sieve and then continue to cook, uncovered, over medium heat for 30 to 45 minutes, or until reduced to 2 quarts. Store in the refrigerator for up to 4 days or freeze for up to 2 months.

Pantry Recipes

PAGE	RECIPE	CALORIES	PROTEIN (g)	
206	Apricot Curry Sauce	10	0	
206	Basil Oil	122	0	
207	Braised Artichokes	55	3	
207	Chicken Stock	30	3	
207	Chocolate Sorbet	30	0	
208	Court Bouillon	40	0	
208	Herb Oil	122	0	
209	Maui Onion Marmalade	50	0	
209	Mushroom Broth	15	0	
209	Preserved Ginger	5	0	
212	Roasted Mushrooms	50	3	
212	Shellfish Stock	20	4	
213	Simple Syrup	45	0	
213	Vegetable Stock	15	0	

COMPLEX CARBOHYDRATES (mg)	FAT (g)	CHOLESTEROL (g)	SATURATED FAT (g)	MONO-UNSATURATED FAT (g)	POLY-UNSATURATED FAT (g)	SODIUM (mg)	FIBER (g)
2	0	0	0	0	0	0	0
0	14	0	1.5	5.5	6.5	0	0
10	0	0	0	0	0	105	5
0	2	5	0	1	0	80	0
7	1.5	0	1	0.5	0	0	0.6
2	0	0	0	0	0	0	0
0	14	0	1.5	5.5	6.5	0	0
9	1.5	0	0.5	1.0	0.5	35	0.6
3	0	0	0	0	0	0	0
1.5	0	0	0	0	0	0	0.1
10	0	0	0	0	0	90	2.5
0	1	5	0	0	0	145	0
12	0	0	0	0	0	0	0
3	0	0	0	0	0	50	0

Charlie Trotter's

816 West Armitage

Chicago, IL 60614 USA

www.charlietrotters.com

One&Only Palmilla

Km 7.5 Carretera Transpeninsular

San Jose Del Cabo

BCS, CP 23400 Mexico

www.oneandonlypalmilla.com

Editor: Sari Zernich, Charlie Trotter's

Research, development, and recipe testing: Sari Zernich, Charlie Trotter's

Copyeditor: Sharon Silva

Proofreader: Rebecca Pepper

Design: Tim Bruce, LOWERCASE, INC.

Project Management: Book Kitchen

Printed in China

ISBN-10: 0-9779890-1-1

ISBN-13: 978-0-9779890-1-0

First printing, 2006

1 2 3 4 5 6 7 8 9 10 — 10 09 08 07 06